William Davies, James Smetham

Letters of James Smetham

Vol. 1

William Davies, James Smetham

Letters of James Smetham
Vol. 1

ISBN/EAN: 9783337017606

Printed in Europe, USA, Canada, Australia, Japan

Cover: Foto ©Thomas Meinert / pixelio.de

More available books at **www.hansebooks.com**

LETTERS

OF THE CELEBRATED

JUNIUS.

A MORE COMPLETE EDITION
THAN ANY YET PUBLISHED.

IN TWO VOLUMES.

VOLUME I.

LONDON:
PRINTED IN THE YEAR M,DCC,LXXXIIL.

ADVERTISEMENT.

THIS edition of the celebrated Letters of Junius, is given as a more complete one than any yet publifhed. In what is called the author's own edition, THREE FOURTHS of the Letter refpecting the Bill of Rights, the moft important one in the collection, were omitted. All thefe omiffions are reftored to their proper places in this edition.

FOURTEEN LETTERS are alfo added to this edition: They are either Letters written by Junius, or Letters to which he has replied; and, on that account, juftice feemed to require, that they fhould be ranged along with his anfwers to them. Thefe Letters are marked with a ftar. A variety of Explanatory Notes have alfo been added; fome of which have been noticed in the contents; but the whole of them were too numerous to be fo diftinguifhed.

IT is proper to obferve, that the Letters figned Philo Junius were written by
                                            Junius,

Junius. In this edition, a miſtake committed in the author's edition has been a-
voided. In that edition, the Letter of Philo
Junius, dated May 22d, 1771, is inſerted
twice; the firſt time in Volume Firſt as a
Note to the twentieth Letter, and the ſecond time in Volume Second, as the forty-
ſixth Letter.

M. DE

LIBERTY of the PRESS.

" WHOEVER considers what it is,
" that constitutes the moving princi-
" ple of what we call great affairs, and the
" invincible sensibility of man to the opinion
" of his fellow-creatures, will not hesitate to
" affirm that, if it were possible for the li-
" berty of the press to exist in a despotic go-
" vernment, and, (what is not less difficult)
" for it to exist without changing the consti-
" tution, this liberty of the press would a-
" lone form a counterpoise to the power of
" the prince. If, for example, in an empire
" of the East, a sanctuary could be found,
" which, rendered respectable by the ancient
" religion of the people, might insure safety
" to those, who should bring thither their
" observations of any kind; and that, from
" thence, printed papers should issue, which
" under a certain seal, might be equally re-
" spected; and which, in their daily appear-
" ance, should examine and freely discuss the
" conduct of the Cadis, the Bashaws, the
" Vizir, the Divan, and the Sultan himself,
" that would introduce immediately some

ERRATUM: Letter **XXXIII.** ſhould be numbered **XXXII.** and Letter **XXXIV.** ſhould be **XXXIII.** and ſo on to the end.

VOLUME FIRST.

a 4   LET-

LET.

L E T-

LET-

LETTERS

LETTERS

OF

JUNIUS, &c.

LETTER I.

TO THE PRINTER OF THE PUBLIC
ADVERTISER.

SIR,   21 *January* 1769.

THE fubmiffion of a free people to
the executive authority of government is no more than a compliance with
laws, which they themfelves have enacted.
While the national honour is firmly maintained abroad, and while juftice is impartially
adminiftered at home, the obedience of the
fubject will be voluntary, chearful, and I
might almoft fay unlimited. A generous
nation is grateful even for the prefervation
of its rights, and willingly extends the refpect
due to the office of a good prince into an
affection for his perfon. Loyalty, in the
heart and underftanding of an Englifhman,
is a rational attachment to the guardian of
the laws. Prejudices and paffion have fometimes carried it to a criminal length; and,
whatever foreigners may imagine, we know
that Englifhmen have erred as much in a

miſtaken zeal for particular perſons and families, as they ever did in defence of what
they thought moſt dear and intereſting to
themſelves.

IT naturally fills us with reſentment, to ſee
ſuch a temper inſulted and abuſed. In reading the hiſtory of a free people, whoſe rights
have been invaded, we are intereſted in
their cauſe. Our own feelings tell us how
long they ought to have ſubmitted, and at
what moment it would have been treachery
to themſelves not to have reſiſted. How
much warmer will be our reſentment, if experience ſhould bring the fatal example home
to ourſelves!

THE ſituation of this country is alarming
enough to rouſe the attention of every man,
who pretends to a concern for the public welfare. Appearances juſtify ſuſpicion; and,
when the ſafety of a nation is at ſtake, ſuſpicion is a juſt ground of enquiry. Let us
enter into it with candour and decency. Reſpect is due to the ſtation of miniſters; and,
if a reſolution muſt at laſt be taken, there is
none ſo likely to be ſupported with firmneſs, as that which has been adopted with
moderation.

THE ruin or proſperity of a ſtate depends
ſo

fo much upon, the adminiſtration of its government, that, to be acquainted with the
merit of a miniſtry, we need only obſerve
the condition of the people. If we ſee
them obedient to the laws, proſperous in
their induſtry, united at home, and re-
ſpected abroad, we may reaſonably preſume that their affairs are conducted by
men of experience, abilities, and virtue. If,
on the contrary, we ſee an univerſal ſpirit of
diſtruſt and diſſatisfaction, a rapid decay
of trade, diſſentions in all parts of the empire, and a total loſs of reſpect in the eyes
of foreign powers, we may pronounce,
without heſitation, that the government of
that country is weak, diſtracted, and corrupt. The multitude, in all countries, are
patient to a certain point. Ill uſage may
rouſe their indignation, and hurry them into exceſſes, but the original fault is in government. Perhaps there never was an inſtance of a change in the circumſtances and
temper of a whole nation, ſo ſudden and
extraordinary as that which the miſconduct
of miniſters has, within theſe few years,
produced in Great Britain. When our
gracious ſovereign aſcended the throne, we
were a flouriſhing and a contented people. If
the perſonal virtues of a king could have
inſured the happineſs of his ſubjects, the
ſcene could not have altered ſo entirely as

it has done. The idea of uniting all parties, of trying all characters, and diftributing the offices of ftate by rotation, was gracious and benevolent to an extreme, though it has not yet produced the many falutary effects which were intended by it. To fay nothing of the wifdom of fuch a plan, it undoubtedly arofe from an unbounded goodnefs of heart, in which folly had no fhare. It was not a capricious partiality to new faces;—it was not a natural turn for low intrigue; nor was it the treacherous amufement of double and triple negotiations. No, Sir, it arofe from a continued anxiety, in the pureft of all poffible hearts, for the general welfare. Unfortunately for us, the event has not been anfwerable to the defign. After a rapid fucceffion of changes we are reduced to that ftate, which hardly any change can mend. Yet there is no extremity of diftrefs, which of itfelf ought to reduce a great nation to defpair. It is not the diforder but the phyfician;—it is not a cafual concurrence of calamitous circumftances, it is the pernicious hand of government, which alone can make a whole people defperate.

WITHOUT much political fagacity, or any extraordinary depth of obfervation, we need only mark how the principal departments of the ftate are beftowed, and look no farther

farther for the true caufe of every mifchief
that befals us.

* THE finances of a nation, finking under
its debts and expences, are committed to a
B 3   young

---

* When the Duke of Grafton firft entered' into
office, it was the fafhion of the times to fuppofe that
young men might have wifdom without experience.
They thought fo themfelves, and the moft important affairs of this country were committed to the firft' trial of
their abilities. His Grace had honourably flefht his
maiden fword in the field of oppofition, and had gone
through all the difcipline of the minority with credit.
He dined at Wildman's, railed at favourites, looked
up to Lord Chatham with aftonifhment, and was the declared advocate of Mr. Wilkes. It afterwards pleafed
his Grace to enter into adminiftration with his friend Lord
Rockingham, and, in a very little time, it pleafed his
Grace to abandon him. He then accepted of the treafury upon terms which Lord Temple had difdained.
For a fhort time his fubmiffion to Lord Chatham was
unlimited. He could not anfwer a private letter without Lord Chatham's permiffion. I prefume he was
then learning his trade, for he foon fet up for himfelf.
Until he declared himfelf the minifter, his character had
been but little underftood. From that moment a fyftem
of conduct, directed by paffion and caprice, not only
reminds us that he is a young man, but a young man
without folidity or judgment. One day he defponds
and threatens to refign. The next, he finds his blood
heated, and fwears to his friend he is determined to go
on. In his public meafures we have feen no proof either of ability or confiftence. The Stamp-act had been
repealed

young nobleman already ruined by play. Introduced to act under the auspices of Lord Chatham, and left at the head of affairs by that nobleman's retreat, he became minister by

repealed (no matter how unwisely) under the preceding administration. The colonies had reason to triumph, and were returning to their good humour. The point was decided, when this young man thought proper to revive it. Without either plan or necessity, he adopts the spirit of Mr. Grenville's measures, and renews the question of taxation in a form more odious and less effectual than that of the law, which had been repealed.

WITH respect to the invasion of Corsica, it will be matter of parliamentary enquiry, whether he has carried on a secret negociation with the French court, in terms contradictory to the resolution of council, and to the instructions drawn up thereupon by his Majesty's secretary of state. If it shall appear that he has quitted the line of his department to betray the honour and security of his country, and if there be a power sufficient to protect him, in such a case, against public justice, the constitution of Great Britain is at an end.

HIS standing foremost in the persecution of Mr. Wilkes, if former declarations and connections be considered, is base and contemptible. The man, whom he now brands with treason and blasphemy, but a very few years ago was the Duke of Grafton's friend, nor is his identity altered, except by his misfortunes.—In the last instance of his Grace's judgment and inconsistency, we see him, after trying and deserting every party, throw himself into the arms of a set of men, whose political principles he had always pretended to abhor.

These

By accident; but deserting the principles and professions, which gave him a moment's popularity, we see him, from every honourable engagement to the public, an apostate by design.

These men I doubt not will teach him the folly of his conduct better than I can. They grasp at every thing, and will soon push him from his seat. His private history would but little deserve our attention, if he had not voluntarily brought it into public notice. I will not call the amusements of a young man criminal, though I think they become his age better than his station. There is a period, at which the most unruly passions are gratified or exhausted, and which leaves the mind clear and undisturbed in its attention to business. His Grace's gallantry would be offended, if we were to suppose him within many years of being thus qualified for public affairs. As for the rest, making every allowance for the frailty of human nature, I can make none for a continued breach of public decorum; nor can I believe that man very zealous for the interest of his country, who sets her opinion at defiance. This nobleman, however, has one claim to respect, since it has pleased our gracious Sovereign to make him prime Minister of Great Britain.

July 10, 1765. The Duke of Grafton took the office of Secretary of State, with an engagement to support the administration of the Marquis of Rockingham, just then formed.

May 23, 1766. He resigned under pretence that he could not act without Mr. Pitt, nor bear to see Mr. Wilkes abandoned; but that under Mr. Pitt he would

act

fign. As for bufinefs, the world yet knows·
nothing of his talents or refolution; unlefs a.
wayward, wavering inconfiftency be a mark of
genius, and caprice a demonftration of fpirit.
It may be faid, perhaps, that it is his Grace's
province, as furely it is his paffion, rather to
diftribute than to fave the public money, and
that while Lord North is Chancellor of the
Exchequer, the Firft Lord of the Treafury
may be as thoughtlefs and extravagant as he
pleafes. I hope however he will not rely too
much on the fertility of Lord North's genius
for finance. His Lordfhip is yet to give us the
firft proof of his abilities: It may be candid
to fuppofe that he has hitherto voluntarily
concealed his talents; intending perhaps to
aftonifh the world, when we leaft expect it,
with a knowledge of trade, a choice of expedients, and a depth of refources, equal to the
neceffities, and far beyond the hopes of his
country. He muft now exert the whole power
of his capacity, if he would wifh us to forget,
that

act in any office. This was the fignal of Lord Rockingham's difmiffion. When Lord Chatham came in, the
Duke got poffeffion of the Treafury.

July 30, 1766. Mr. Pitt was created Earl of Chatham, and appointed Lord Privy Seal.

August 2, 1766. The Duke of Grafton was appointed Firft Lord of the Treafury, in room of the
Marquis of Rockingham.

that since he has been in office, no plan has been formed, no fyftem adhered to, nor any one important meafure adopted for the relief of public credit. If his plan for the fervice of the current year be not irrevocably fixed on, let me warn him to think ferioufly of confequences before he ventures to increafe the public debt. Outraged and oppreffed as we are, this nation will not bear, after a fix years peace, to fee new millions borrowed, without an eventual diminution of debt, or reduction of intereft. The attempt might roufe a fpirit of refentment, which might reach beyond the facrifice of a minifter. As to the debt upon the civil lift, the people of England expect that it will not be paid without a ftrict enquiry how it was incurred. If it muft be paid by parliament, let me advife the Chancellor of the Exchequer to think of fome better expedient than a lottery. To fupport an expenfive war, or in circumftances of abfolute neceffity, a lottery may perhaps be allowable; but, befides that it is at all times the very worft way of raifing money upon the people, I think it ill becomes the Royal dignity to have the debts of a King provided for, like the repairs of a country bridge, or a decayed hofpital. The management of the King's affairs in the Houfe of Commons cannot be more difgraced than it has been. * A

B 5

lead-

* Lord North.

leading Minifter repeatedly called down for abfolute ignorance ;—ridiculous motions ridiculoufly withdrawn ;—deliberate plans difconcerted, and a week's preparation of graceful oratory loft in a moment, give us fome, though not an adequate idea of Lord North's parliamentary abilities and influence. Yet before he had the misfortune of being Chancellor of the Exchequer, he was neither an object of derifion to his enemies, nor of melancholy pity to his friends.

A SERIES of inconfiftent meafures has alienated the colonies from their duty as fubjects, and from their nàtural affection to their common country. When Mr. Grenville was placed at the head of the Treafury, he felt the impoffibility of Great Britain's fupporting fuch an eftablifhment as her former fuccefles had made indifpenfable, and at the fame time of giving any fenfible relief to foreign trade, and to the weight of the public debt. He thought it equitable that thofe parts of the empire, which had benefited moft by the expences of the war, fhould contribute fomething to the expences of the peace, and he had no doubt of the conftitutional right vefted in parliament to raife the contribution. But, unfortunately for this country, Mr. Grenville was at any rate to be diftreffed becaufe he was Minifter, and Mr. Pitt and Lord Camden

were

were to be the patrons of America, becaufe they were in oppofition. Their declamation gave fpirit and argument to the colonies, and while perhaps they meant no more than a ruin of a minifter, they in effect divided one half of the empire from the other*.

UNDER one adminiftration the ftamp act is made†; under the fecond it is repealed‡; under the third, in fpite of all experience, a new mode of taxing the colonies is invented§, and a queftion revived, which ought to have been buried in oblivion. In thefe circumftances a new office is eftablifhed for the bufinefs of the plantations, and the Earl of Hillfborough called forth, at a moft critical

---

* THIS, though faid upwards of *fix years* before the war, has turned out too true a prophecy. It is worthy of remark that two great characters, who were very far from being attached to each other, yet thought nearly alike on the American bufinefs. Lord Mansfield, two years before the above letter was written, in a fpeech againft the fufpending and difpenfing prerogative, reminded the Houfe of what had been told them the year before, " *that they would import rebellion from America.*"

† GRENVILLE Adminiftration.

‡ ROCKINGHAM Adminiftration.

§ The tea duty laid by the Chatham and Grafton Adminiftration.

feafon.

feafon, to govern America. The choice at
leaft announced to us a man of fuperior capacity and knowledge. Whether he be fo or
not, let his difpatches as far as they have appeared, let his meafures as far as they have
operated, determine for him. In the former
we have feen ftrong affertions without proof,
declamation without argument, and violent
cenfures without dignity or moderation; but
neither correctnefs in the compofition, nor
judgment in the defign. As for his meafures, let it be remembered, that he was called
upon to conciliate and unite; and that, when
he entered into office, the moft refractory of
the colonies were ftill difpofed to proceed by
the conftitutional methods of petition and
remonftrance. Since that period they have
been driven into exceffes little fhort of rebellion. Petitions have been hindered from
reaching the throne; and the continuance of
one of the principal affemblies refted upon an
arbitrary condition§, which, confidering the
temper they were in, it was impoffible they
fhould comply with, and which would have
availed nothing as to the general queftion, if
it had been complied with. So violent, and
I believe I may call it fo unconftitutional an
exertion of the prerogative, to fay nothing of

§ That they fhould retract one of their refolutions,
and erafe the entry of it.

the

the weak, injudicious terms in which it was conveyed, gives us as humble an opinion of his lordſhip's capacity, as it does of his temper and moderation. While we are at peace with other nations, our military force may perhaps be ſpared to ſupport the Earl of Hillſborough's meaſures in America. Whenever that force ſhall be neceſſarily withdrawn or diminiſhed, the diſmiſſion of ſuch a miniſter will neither conſole us for his imprudence, nor remove the ſettled reſentment of a people, who, complaining of an act of the legiſlature, are outraged by an unwarrantable ſtretch of prerogative, and, ſupporting their claims by argument, are inſulted with declamation.

Drawing lots would be a prudent and reaſonable method of appointing the officers of ſtate, compared to a late diſpoſition of the ſecretary's office. Lord Rochford was acquainted with the affairs and temper of the ſouthern courts: Lord Weymouth was equally qualified for either department*. By what unaccountable caprice has it happened, that the latter, who pretends to no experience what-

---

* It was ſaid, that this remove was made out of compliment to the Duke of Choiſeuil, the French Miniſter, as Lord Rochford, when Ambaſſador in France, had offended his Grace by ſome ſpirited repreſentations.

ſoever

foever, is removed to the moſt important of the two departments, and the former by preference placed in an office, where his experience can be of no uſe to him ? Lord Weymouth had diſtinguiſhed himſelf in his firſt employment by a ſpirited if not judicious conduct. He had animated the civil magiſtrate beyond the tone of civil authority, and had directed the operations of the army to more than military execution. Recovered from the errors of his youth, from the diſtraction of play, and the bewitching ſmiles of Burgundy, behold him exerting the whole ſtrength of his clear, unclouded faculties, in the ſervice of the crown. It was not the heat of midnight exceſſes, nor ignorance of the laws, nor furious ſpirit of the houſe of Bedford; No, Sir, when this reſpectable miniſter interpoſed his authority between the magiſtrate, and the people, and ſigned the mandate, on which, for aught he knew, the lives of thouſands depended, he did it from the deliberate motion of his heart, ſupported by the beſt of his judgment.

IT has lately been a faſhion to pay a compliment to the bravery and generoſity of the commander in chief*, at the expence of his underſtanding. They who love him leaſt make no queſtion of his courage, while his

* The late Marquis of Granby.

friends

friends dwell chiefly on the facility of his difpofition. Admitting him to be as brave as a total abfence of all feeling and reflection can make him, let us fee what fort of merit he derives from the remainder of his character. If it be generofity to accumulate in his own perfon and family a number of lucrative employments; to provide, at the public expence, for every creature that bears the name of Manners; and, neglecting the merit and fervices of the reft of the army, to heap promotions upon his favourites and dependants, the prefent commander in chief is the moft generous man alive. Nature has been fparing of her gifts to this noble lord; but where birth and fortune are united, we expect the noble pride and independence of a man of fpirit, not the fervile, humiliating complaifance of a courtier. As to the goodnefs of his heart, if a proof of it be taken from the facility of never refufing, what conclufion fhall we draw from the indecency of never performing? And if the difcipline of the army be in any degree preferved, what thanks are due to a man, whofe cares, notorioufly confined to filling up vacancies, have degraded the office of commander in chief into a broker of commiffions*!

* Thefe animadverfions brought forward Sir William Draper, who though poffeffed of great literary talents, could not cope with Junius.

WITH

WITH respect to the navy, I shall only say, that this country is so highly indebted to Sir Edward Hawke, that no expence should be spared to secure to him an honourable and affluent retreat..

THE pure and impartial administration of justice is perhaps the firmest bond to secure a chearful submission of the people, and to engage their affections to government. It is not sufficient that questions of private right or wrong are justly decided, nor that judges are superior to the vileness of pecuniary corruption. Jefferies himself, when the court had no interest, was an upright judge. A court of justice may be subject to another sort of bias, more important and pernicious, as it reaches beyond the interest of individuals, and affects the whole community. A judge under the influence of government, may be honest enough in the decision of private causes, yet a traitor to the public. When a victim is marked out by the ministry, this judge will offer himself to perform the sacrifice.. He will not scruple to prostitute his dignity, and betray the sanctity of his office, whenever an arbitrary point is to be carried for government, or the resentment of a court to be gratified.

THESE

THESE principles and proceedings, odious and contemptible as they are, in effect are no lefs injudicious. A wife and generous people are roufed by every appearance of oppreffive, unconftitutional meafures, whether thofe meafures are fupported only by the power of government, or mafked under the forms of a court of juftice. Prudence and felf-prefervation will oblige the moft moderate difpofitions to make it a common caufe, even with a man whofe conduct they cenfure, if they fee him perfecuted in a way, which the real fpirit of the laws will not juftify. The facts, on which thefe remarks are founded, are too notorious to require an application.

THIS, Sir, is the detail. In one view behold a nation overwhelmed with debt; her revenues wafted; her trade declining; the affections of her colonies alienated; the duty of the magiftrate transferred to the foldiery; a gallant army, which never fought unwillingly but againft their fellow fubjects, mouldering away for want of the direction of a man of common abilities and fpirit; and, in the laft inftance, the adminiftration of juftice become odious and fufpected to the whole body of the people. This deplorable fcene admits of but one addition---that we are governed by counfels, from which a rea-

fonable

fonable man can expect no remedy but poifon, no relief but death.

IF, by the immediate interpofition of Providence, it were poffible for us to efcape a
crifis fo full of terror and defpair, pofterity
will not believe the hiftory of the prefent
times. They will either conclude that our
diftreffes were imaginary, or that we had
the good fortune to be governed by men of acknowledged integrity and wifdom : they will
not believe it poffible that their anceftors
could have furvived, or recovered from fo defperate a condition, while a Duke of Grafton
was Prime Minifter, a Lord North Chancellor of the Exchequer, a Weymouth and a
Hillfborough Secretaries of State, a Granby
Commander in Chief, and a Mansfield chief
criminal Judge of the kingdom.

JUNIUS.

LETTER

L E T T E R II.

TO THE PRINTER OF THE PUBLIC AD-
VERTISER.

'S I R,   26 *January*, 1769.

T H.E kingdom fwarms with fuch numbers of felonious robbers of private
character and virtue, that no honeft or
good man is fafe; efpecially as thefe cow-
ardly bafe affaffins ftab in the dark, without
having the courage to fign their real names
to their malevolent and wicked productions:
A writer, who figns himfelf Junius, in the
Public Advertifer of the 21ft inftant, opens
the deplorable fituation of his country in
a very affecting manner; with a pompous
parade of his candour and decency, he tells
us, that we fee diffentions in all parts of the
empire, an univerfal fpirit of diftruft and dif-
fatisfaction, and a total lofs of refpect towards
us in the eyes of foreign powers. But this
writer, with all his boafted candour, has not
told us the real caufe of the evils he fo pa-
thetically enumerates. I fhall take the liberty
to explain the caufe for him. Junius, and
fuch writers as himfelf, occafion all the mifchief complained of, by falfely and malici-
oufly

oufly traducing the beft charaƈters in the kingdom. For when our deluded people at home, and foreigners abroad, read the poifonous and inflammatory libels that are daily publifhed with impunity, to vilify thofe who are any way diftinguifhed by their good qualities and eminent virtues : when they find no notice taken of, or reply given to thefe flanderous tongues and pens, their conclufion is, that both the minifters and the nation have been fairly defcribed; and they aƈt accordingly. I think it therefore the duty of every good citizen to ftand forth, and endeavour to undeceive the public, when the vileft arts are made ufe of to defame and blacken the brighteft charaƈters among us. An eminent author affirms it to be almoft as criminal to hear a worthy man traduced, without attempting his juftification, as to be the author of the calumny againft him. For my own part, I think it a fort of mifprifion of treafon againft fociety. No man therefore who knows Lord Granby, can poffibly hear fo good and great a charaƈter moft vilely, abufed, without a warm and juft indignation againft this Junius, this high-prieft of envy, malice, and all uncharitablenefs, who has endeavoured to facrifice our beloved commander in chief at the altars of his horrid deities. Nor is the injury done to his lordfhip alone, but to the whole nation, which may

too

too foon feel the contempt, and confequently the attacks of our late enemies, if they can be induced to believe that the perfon, on whom the fafety of thefe kingdoms fo much depends, is unequal to his high ftation, and deftitute of thofe qualities which form a good general. One would have thought that his lordfhip's fervices in the caufe of his country, from the battle of Culloden to his moft glorious conclufion of the late war, might have entitled him to common refpect and decency at leaft; but this uncandid indecent writer has gone fo far as to turn one of the moft amiable men of the age into a ftupid, unfeeling, and fenfelefs being; poffeffed indeed of a perfonal courage, but void of thofe effential qualities which diftinguifh the commander from the common foldier.

A very long, uninterrupted, impartial, I will add, a moft difinterefted friendfhip with Lord Granby, gives me the right to affirm, that all Junius's affertions are falfe and fcandalous. Lord Granby's courage, though of the brighteft and moft ardent kind, is among the loweft of his numerous good qualities; he was formed to excel in war by nature's liberality to his mind as well as perfon. Educated and inftructed by his moft noble father, and a moft fpirited as well as excellent fcholar, the prefent Bifhop of Bangor,

gor, he was trained to the nicest sense of honour, and to the truest and noblest sort of
pride, that of never doing or suffering a
mean action. A sincere love and attachment
to his king and country, and to their glory,
first impelled him to the field, where he never
gained aught but honour. He impaired,
through his bounty, his own fortune; for
his bounty, which this writer would in vain
depreciate, is founded upon the noblest of the
human affections, it flows from a heart melt-
ing to goodness from the most refined humanity. Can a man, who is described as unfeeling, and void of reflection, be constantly
employed in seeking proper objects on whom
to exercise those glorious virtues of compas-
sion and generosity? The distressed officer,
the soldier, the widow, the orphan, and a
long list besides, know that vanity has no
share in his frequent donations: he gives,
because he feels their distresses. Nor has he
ever been rapacious with one hand to be
bountiful with the other; yet this uncandid
Junius would insinuate, that the dignity of
the commander in chief is depraved into the
base office of a commission broker; that is,
Lord Granby bargains for the sale of com-
missions; for it must have this meaning, if
it has any at all. But where is the man liv-
ing who can justly charge his lordship with
such mean practices? Why does not Junius
produce

produce him ? Junius knows that he has no other means of wounding this hero, than from fome miffile weapon, fhot from an obfcure corner : He feeks, as all fuch defamatory writers do,

> *fpargere voces*
> *In Vulgum ambiguas,*

'to raife fufpicion in the minds of the people. But I hope that my countrymen will be no longer impofed upon by artful and defigning men, or by wretches, who, bankrupts in bufinefs, in fame, and in fortune, mean nothing more than to involve this country in the fame common ruin with themfelves. Hence it is, that they are conftantly aiming their dark and too often fatal weapons againft thofe who ftand forth as the bulwark of our national fafety. Lord Granby was too confpicuous a mark not to be their object. He is next attacked for being unfaithful to his promifes and engagements : Where are Junius's proofs ? Although I could give fome inftances, where a breach of promife would be a virtue, efpecially in the cafe of thofe who would pervert the open, unfufpecting moments of convivial mirth, into fly, infidious applications for preferment, or party fyftems, and would endeavour to furprife a good man, who cannot bear to fee any one leave him diffatisfied, diſſatisfied, into unguarded promiſes. Lord Granby's attention to his own family and relations is called ſelfiſh. Had he not attended to them, when fair and juſt opportunities preſented themſelves, I ſhould have thought him unfeeling, and void of reflection indeed. How are any man's friends or relations to be provided for, but from the influence and protection of the patron? It is unfair to ſuppoſe that Lord Granby's friends have not as much merit as the friends of any other great man: If he is generous at the public expence, as Junius invidiouſly calls it, the public is at no more expence for his lordſhip's friends, than it would be if any other ſet of men poſſeſſed thoſe offices. The charge is ridiculous!

THE laſt charge againſt Lord Granby is of a moſt ſerious and alarming nature indeed. Junius aſſerts, that the army is mouldering away for want of the direction of a man of common abilities and ſpirit, The preſent condition of the army gives the directeſt lie to his aſſertions. It was never upon a more reſpectable footing with regard to diſcipline, and all the eſſentials that can form good ſoldiers. Lord Ligonier delivered a firm and noble palladium of our ſafeties into Lord Granby's hands, who has kept it in the ſame good order in which he received it. The

ſtricteſt

ftricteft care has been taken to fill up the vacant commiffions, with fuch gentlemen as
have the glory of their anceftors to fupport,
as well as their own, and are doubly bound
to the caufe of their king and country, from
motives of private property, as well as public fpirit. The adjutant-general, who has
the immediate care of the troops after Lord
Granby, is an officer that would do great honour in any fervice in Europe, for his correct
arrangements, good fenfe and difcernment
upon all occafions, and for a punctuality
and precifion which give the moft entire fatisfaction to all who are obliged to confult
him. The reviewing generals, who infpect
the army twice a year, have been felected
with the greateft care, and have anfwered
the important truft repofed in them in the
moft laudable manner. Their reports of
the condition of the army are much more
to be credited than thofe of Junius, whom
I do advife, to atone for his fhameful afperfions, by afking pardon of Lord Granby and the whole kingdom, whom he has
offended by his abominable fcandals. In
fhort, to turn Junius's own battery againft
him, I muft affert, in his own words, " that
he has given ftrong affertions without
proof, declamation without argument, and

VOL. I.   C   violent

violent cenfures without dignity or moderation."

WILLIAM DRAPER*.

LETTER

* SIR WILLIAM DRAPER diftinguifhed himfelf laft
war, in the Eaft Indies, during the fiege of Madras by
the French ; and he commanded in chief at the taking of
Manilla.   When he was made a Knight of the Bath,
he was fo enamoured with the honour, that he had
the ftar embroidered even on his night-gown.   After
his literary warfare with Junius; he went abroad on a
tour through the Englifh Colonies on the Continent
of America.   On the commencement of the prefent
war, he was appointed Lieutenant Governor of Mi-
norca, and ferved during the late fiege of St. Philips
under Lieutenant General Murray, the Governor of the
Ifland.   He has ftill an unfettled difpute with that
officer.

———————

A FEW days after his firft letter to Junius, Sir William publifhed the following curious, but well meant
addrefs to the public :

Clifton, Feb. 6, 1769.

IF the voice of a well meaning individual could be
heard amid the clamour, fury, and madnefs of the
times, would it appear too rafh and prefumptuous to
propofe to the public, than an act of indemnity and
oblivion may be made for all paft tranfactions and offences, as well with refpect to Mr. Wilkes as to our
colonies ?   Such falutary expedients have been em-
braced by the wifeft nations ; fuch expedients have
been made ufe of by our own, when the public confu-
fions had arrived to fome very dangerous and alarming
crifis ; and I believe it needs not the gift of prophecy to
foretel

LETTER III.

TO SIR WILLIAM DRAPER, KNIGHT OF THE BATH.

S I R,   7 *February*, 1769.

YOUR defence of Lord Granby does. honour · to the goodnefs of your heart. You feel as you ought to do, for the reputation of your friend, and you exprefs yourfelf in the

C 2   warmeft.

foretel, that fome fuch crifis is now approaching. Perhaps it will be more wife and praife-worthy to make fuch an act immediately, in order to prevent the poffibility, not to fay the probability of an infurrection at home, and in our dependencies abroad, than it will be to be obliged to have recourfe to one after the mifchief has been done, and the kingdom has groaned under all the miferies that avarice, ambition, hypocrify, and madnefs could inflict upon it. An act of grace, indemnity, and oblivion, was paffed upon the reftoration of king Charles II. but I will venture to fay, that had fuch an act been feafonably paffed in the reign of his unhappy father, the civil war had been prevented, and no reftoration had been neceffary. It is too late to recal·the meffengers and edicts of wrath! Cannot the money that is now wafted in endlefs and mutual profecutions, and in ftopping the mouth of one man, and in opening that of another, be better employed in ·erecting a temple to concord ? Let Mr. Wilkes lay the firft ftone, and fuch a

ftone

warmest language of your paſſions. In any other cauſe, I doubt not, you would have cautiouſly weighed the conſequences of committing your name to the licentious diſcourſes and malignant opinions of the world. But here, I preſume, you thought it would be a breach of friendſhip to loſe one moment in conſulting your underſtanding; as if an appeal to the public were no more than a military *coup de main*, where a brave man has no rules to follow, but the dictates of his courage. Touched with your generoſity, I freely forgive the exceſſes into which it has led you; and, far from reſenting thoſe terms of reproach, which, conſidering that you are an advocate for decorum, you have heaped upon me rather too liberally, I place them to the account of an honeſt unreflecting indignation, in which your cooler judgment and natural politeneſs had no concern. I approve of the ſpirit, with which you have given your name

ſtone as I hope the builders will not refuſe. May this Parliament, to uſe Lord Clarendon's expreſſion, be called *The Healing Parliament!* May our foul wounds be cleanſed and then cloſed! The Engliſh have been as famous for good-nature as for valour; let it not be ſaid that ſuch qualities are degenerated into ſavage ferocity. If any of my friends in either houſe of legiſlature ſhall condeſcend to liſten to, and improve theſe hints, I ſhall think that I have not lived in vain.

WILLIAM DRAPER.

to the public; and, if it were a proof of any thing but fpirit, I fhould have thought myfelf bound to follow your example. I fhould have hoped that even *my* name might carry fome authority with it, if. I had not feen how very little weight or confideration a printed. paper receives even from the refpectable fignature of Sir William Draper.

You begin with a general affertion, that writers, fuch as I am, are the real caufe of all the public evils we complain of. And do you really think, Sir William, that the licentious pen of a political writer is able to produce fuch important effects? A little calm reflection might have fhewn you, that national calamities do not arife from the defcription, but from the real character and conduct of minifters. To have fupported your affertion, you fhould have proved that the prefent. miniftry are unqueftionably the *beft and brighteft* characters of the kingdom ; and that, if the affections of the colonies have been alienated, if Corfica has been fhamefully abandoned, if commerce. languifhes, if public credit is threatened with a new debt, and your own Manilla ranfom moft difhonourably given up, it has all been owing to the malice of political writers, who will not fuffer the beft and brighteft of characters (meaning ftill the prefent miniftry) to take a

fingle

fingle right ftep for the honour or intereft of the nation. But it feems you were a little tender of coming to particulars. Your con-fcience infinuated to you that it would be prudent to leave the characters of Grafton, North, Hillfborough, Weymouth, and Manf-field, to fhift for themfelves; and, truly, Sir William, the part you *have* undertaken is at leaft as much as you are equal to.

Without difputing Lord Granby's cou-rage, we are yet to learn in what articles of military knowledge nature has been fo very liberal to his mind. If you have ferved with him, you ought to have pointed out fome in-ftances of able difpofition and well-concerted enterprize, which might fairly be attributed to his capacity as a general. It is you, Sir William, who make your friend appear auk-ward and ridiculous, by giving him a laced fuit of tawdry qualifications, which nature never intended him to wear.

You fay, he has acquired nothing but ho-nour in the field. Is the Ordnance nothing? Are the Blues nothing? Is the command of the army, with all the patronage annexed to it, nothing? Where he got thefe *nothings* I know not; but you at leaft ought to have told us where he deferved them.

As

As to his bounty, compaffion, &c. it would have been but little to the purpofe, though you had proved all that you have afferted. I meddle with nothing but his charaćter as commander in chief; and, though I acquit him of the bafenefs of felling commiffions, I ftill affert that his military cares have never extended beyond the difpofal of vacancies; and I am juftified by the complaints of the whole army, when I fay that, in this diftribution, he confults nothing but parliamentary interefts, or the gratification of his immediate dependants. As to his fervile fubmiffion to the reigning miniftry, let me afk, whether he did not defert the caufe of the whole army, when he fuffered Sir Jeffery Amherft to be facrificed, and what fhare he had in recalling that officer to the fervice? Did he not betray the juft intereft of the army, in permitting Lord Percy to have a regiment? And does he not at this moment give up all charaćter and dignity as a gentleman, in receding from his own repeated declarations in favour of Mr. Wilkes?

In the two next articles I think we are agreed. You candidly admit, that he often makes fuch promifes as it is a virtue in him to violate, and that no man is more affiduous to provide for his relations at the public expence. I did not urge the laft as an abfolute

C 4   vice

vice in his difpofition, but to prove that a
carelefs difinterefted spirit is no part of his character; and as to the other, I defire it may
be remembered, that *I* never defcended to
the indecency of enquiring into his *convivial
hours.* It is you, Sir William Draper, who
have taken pains to reprefent your friend in
the character of a drunken landlord, who
deals out his promifes as liberally as his liquor, and will fuffer no man to leave his
table either forrowful or fober. None but
an intimate friend, who muft frequently have
feen him in thefe unhappy, difgraceful moments could have defcribed him fo well.

THE laft charge, of the neglect of the
army, is indeed the moft material of all. I
am forry to tell you, Sir William, that, in
this article, your firft fact is falfe, and as there
is nothing more painful to me than to give a
direct contradiction to a gentleman of your
appearance, I could wifh that, in your future
publications, you would pay a greater attention to the truth of your premifes, before
you fuffer your genius to hurry you to a conclufion. Lord Ligonier *did not* deliver the
army (which you, in claffical language, are
pleafed to call a palladium) into Lord
Granby's hands. It was taken from him
much againft his inclination, fome two or
three years before Lord Granby was commander

mandèr in chief. As to the ftate of the army, I fhould be glad to know where you have received your intelligence. Was it in the rooms at Bath, or at your retreat at Clifton? The reports of reviewing generals comprehend only a few regiments in England, which, as they are immediately under the royal infpection, are perhaps in fome tolerable order. But do you know any thing of the troops in the Weft Indies, the Mediterranean, and North America, to fay nothing of a whole army abfolutely ruined in Ireland? Inquire a little into facts, Sir William, before you publifh your next panegyric upon Lord Granby, and believe me you will find there is a fault at head-quarters, which even the acknowledged care and abilities of the adjutant general cannot correct.

PERMIT me now, Sir William, to addrefs myfelf perfonally to you, by way of thanks for the honour of your correfpondence. You are by no means undeferving of notice; and it may be of confequence even to Lord Granby to have it determined, whether or no the man, who has praifed him fo lavifhly, be himfelf deferving of praife. When you returned to Europe, you zealoufly undertook the caufe of that gallant army, by whofe bravery at Manilla your own fortune had been efta-

blifhed.

blifhed.   You complained, you threatened,
you even appealed to the public in print.
By what accident did it happen, that in the
midft of all this buftle, and all thefe clamours
for juftice to your injured troops, the name
of the Manilla ranfom was fuddenly buried
in a profound, and, fince that time, an uninterrupted filence ? Did the Miniftry fuggeft
any motives to you ftrong enough to tempt
a man of honour to defert and betray the caufe
of his fellow-foldiers ? Was it that blufhing
ribband, which is now the perpetual ornament of your perfon? Or was it that regiment, which you afterwards (a thing unpre-
cedented among foldiers) fold to colonel Gifborne ? Or was it that government, the full
pay of which you are contented to hold, with
the half-pay of an Irifh colonel ? And do
you now, after a retreat not very like that
of Scipio, prefume to intrude yourfelf, un-
thought-of, uncalled for, upon the patience
of the public ? Are your flatteries of the
commander in chief directed to another regiment, which you may again difpofe of on
the fame honourable terms ? We know your
prudence, Sir William, and I fhould be forry
to ftop your preferment.

                              JUNIUS.

LETTER IV.

TO JUNIUS.

SIR, 17 *February* 1769.

I RECEIVED Junius's favour laſt night; he is determined to keep his advantage by the help of his maſk; it is an excellent protection, it has faved many a man from an untimely end.. But whenever he will be honeſt enough to lay it aſide, avow himſelf, and produce the face which has ſo long lurked behind it, the world will be able to judge of his motives for writing ſuch infamous invectives. His real name will difcover his freedom and independency, or his fervility to a faction. Difappointed ambition, refentment for defeated hopes, and defire of revenge, aſſume but too often the appearance of public ſpirit; but be his defigns wicked or charitable, Junius ſhould learn that it is poſſible to condemn meafures, without a barbarous and criminal outrage againſt men. Junius delights to mangle carcaſes with a hatchet; his language and inſtrument have a great connexion with Clare Market, and, to do him juſtice, he handles his weapon moſt admirably. One would imagine he had been taught

C 6 to

to throw it by the favages of America. It
is therefore high time for me to ftep in once
more to fhield my friend from this mercilefs
weapon, although I may be wounded in the
attempt. But I muft firft afk Junius by
what forced analogy and conftruction the
moments of convivial mirth are made to fignify indecency, a-violation of engagements,
a drunken landford, and a defire that every
one in company fhould be drunk likewife?
He muft have culled all the flowers of St.
Giles's and Billingfgate to have produced
fuch a piece of oratory. Here the hatchet
defcends with tenfold vengeance; but, alas!
it hurts no one but its mafter! For
Junius muft not think to put words into
my mouth, that feem too foul even for his
own.

My friend's political engagements I know
not, fo cannot pretend to explain them, or
affert their confiftency. I know not whether
Junius be confiderable enough to belong to
any party; if he fhould be fo, can he affirm
that he has always adhered to one fet of men
and meafures? Is he fure that he has never
fided with thofe whom he was firft hired to
abufe? Has he never abufed thofe he was
hired to praife? To fay the truth, moft men's
politics fit much too loofely about them.
But as my friend's military character was
                                                 the

the chief object that engaged me in this controverfy, to that I fhall return..

Junius afks what inftances my friend has
given of his military fkill and capacity as a
general? When and where he gained his honour? When he deferved his emoluments?
The united voice of the army which ferved
under him, the glorious teftimony of prince
Ferdinand, and of vanquifhed enemies, all
Germany will tell him. Junius repeats the
complaints of the army againft parliamentary
influence. I love the army too well, not to
wifh that fuch influence were lefs. Let Junius point out the time when it has not prevailed. It was of the leaft force in the time
of that great man, the late duke of Cumberland, who, as a prince of the blood, was
able as well as willing to ftem a torrent which
would have overborne any private fubject. In
time of war this influence is fmall. In peace,
when difcontent and faction have the fureft
means to operate, efpecially in this country,
and when, from a fcarcity of public fpirit, the
wheels of government are rarely moved, but
by the power and force of obligations, its
weight is always too great. Yet, if this influence at prefent has done no greater harm
than the placing Earl Percy at the head of a
regiment, I do not think that either the rights
or beft interefts of the army are facrificed and
betrayed,

betrayed, or the nation undone. Let me ask
Junius, if he knows any one nobleman in the
army, who has had a regiment by seniority?
I feel myself happy in seeing young noblemen of illustrious name and great property come among us. They are an additional
security to the kingdom from foreign or do-
mestic slavery. Junius needs not be told, that
should the time ever come, when this nation
is to be defended only by those, who have
nothing more to lose than their arms and
their pay, its danger will be great indeed. A
happy mixture of men of quality with soldiers of fortune is always to be wished for.
But the main point is still to be contended
for, I mean the discipline and condition of
the army, and I must still maintain, though
contradicted by Junius, that it was never
upon a more respectable footing, as to all the
essentials that can form good soldiers, than it
is at present. Junius is forced to allow that
our army at home may be in some tolerable
order ; yet how kindly does he invite our late
enemies to the invasion of Ireland, by assuring
them that the army in that kingdom is totally
ruined ! (The colonels of that army are
much obliged to him) I have too great an
opinion of the military talents of the lord
lieutenant, and of all their diligence and capacity, to believe it. If from some strange,
unaccountable fatality, the people of that
kingdom

kingdom cannot be induced to confult their own fecurity, by fuch an effectual augmenta-, tion, as may enable the troops there to act with power and energy, is the commander in chief here to blame ? Or is he to blame, be- caufe the troops in the Mediterranean, in the Weft-Indies, in America, labour under great difficulties from the fcarcity of men, which is but too vifible all over thefe king- doms ! Many of our forces are in climates unfavourable to Britifh conftitutions : their lofs is in proportion. Britain muft recruit all thefe regiments from her own emaciated bofom, or more precarioufly, by catholicks from Ireland. We are likewife fubject to the- fatal drains to the Eaft-Indies, to Senegal, and the alarming emigrations of our people to other countries: Such depopulation can only be repaired by a long peace, or by fome fenfible bill of naturalization.

I MUST now take the liberty to talk to Junius on my own account. He is pleafed to tell me that he addreffes himfelf to me perfonally, I fhall be glad to fee him. It is his imperfonality that I complain of, and his invifible attacks ; for his dagger in the air is only to be regarded, becaufe one cannot fee the hand which holds it ; but had it not wounded other people more deeply than my-

felf,

felf, I fhould not have obtruded myfelf at all
on the patience of the public.

MARK how a plain tale fhall put him
down, and transfufe the blufh of my ribband
into his own cheeks. Junius tells me, that
at my return, I zealoufly undertook the caufe
of the gallant army, by whofe bravery at Manilla my own fortunes were eftablifhed; that
I complained, that I even appealed to the
public. I did fo; I glory in having done fo,
as I had an undoubted right to vindicate my
own character, attacked by a Spanifh memorial, and to affert the rights of my brave companions. I glory likewife, that I have never
taken up my pen, but to vindicate the injured. Junius afks by what accident did it
happen, that in the midft of all this buftle,
and all the clamours for juftice to the injured
troops, the Manilla ranfom was fuddenly buried in a profound, and, fince that time, an
uninterrupted filence? I will explain the
caufe to the public. The feveral minifters
who have been employed fince that time have
been very defirous to do juftice from two
moft laudable motives, a ftrong inclination
to affift injured bravery, and to acquire a well
deferved popularity to themfelves. Their efforts have been in vain. Some were ingenu-
ous enough to own, that they could not
think of involving this diftreffed nation into
another

another war for our private concerns. In short, our rights for the prefent are facrificed to national convenience; and I muft confefs, that although I may lofe five-and-twenty thoufand pounds by their acquiefcence to this breach of faith in the Spaniards, I think they are in the right to temporize, confidering the critical fituation of this country, convulfed in every part by poifon infufed by anonymous, wicked, and incendiary writers. Lord Shelburne will do me the juftice to own, that, in September laft, I waited upon him with a joint memorial from the admiral Sir S. Cornifh and myfelf, in behalf of our injured companions. His lordfhip was as frank upon the occafion as other fecretaries had been before him. He did not deceive us by giving any immediate hopes of relief.

Junius would bafely infinuate, that my filence may have been purchafed by my government, by my *blufhing* ribband, by my regiment, by the fale of that regiment, and by half-pay as an Irifh colonel.

His Majefty was pleafed to give me my government, for my fervice at Madras. I had my firft regiment in 1757. Upon my return from Manilla, his Majefty, by Lord Egremont, informed me, that I fhould have the firft vacant red ribband, as a reward for

many

many fervices in an enterprize, which I had
planned as well as executed. The Duke of
Bedford and Mr. Grenville confirmed thofe
affurances many months before the Spaniards
had protefted the ranfom bills. To accommodate Lord Clive, then going upon a moft
important fervice to Bengal, I waved my
claim to the vacancy which then happened.
As there was no other vacancy until the Duke
of Grafton and Lord Rockingham were joint
minifters, I was then honoured with the order, and it is furely no fmall honour to me,
that in fuch a fucceffion of minifters, they
were all pleafed to think that I had deferved
it; in my favour they were all united. Upon the reduction of the 79th regiment, which
had ferved fo glorioufly in the Eaft-Indies, his
Majefty, unfolicited by me, gave me the
16th of foot as an equivalent. My motives
for retiring afterwards are foreign to the
purpofe ; let it fuffice, that his Majefty
was pleafed to approve of them ; they are
fuch as no man can think indecent, who
knows the fhocks that repeated viciffitudes of
heat and cold, of dangerous and fickly climates, will give to the beft conftitutions in a
pretty long courfe of fervice. I refigned my
regiment to colonel Gifborne, a very good
officer, for his half-pay, 120ol. Irifh annuity; fo that, according to Junius, I have
been bribed to fay nothing more of the Manilla

nilla ranfom, and facrifice thofe brave men
by the ftrange avarice of accepting three
hundred and eighty pounds per ann. and giving up eight hundred! If this be bribery, it
is not the bribery of thefe times. As to my
flattery, thofe who know me will judge of it.
By the afperity of Junius's ftile, I cannot indeed call him a flatterer, unlefs he be as a
cynick or a maftiff: if he wags his tail, he
will ftill growl, and long to bite. The public will now judge of the credit that ought to
be given to Junius's writings, from the falfi-
ties that he has infinuated with refpect to
myfelf.

WILLIAM DRAPER.

LETTER V.

TO SIR WILLIAM DRAPER, KNIGHT
OF THE BATH.

S I R,   21 *February*, 1769.

I SHOULD juftly be fufpected of acting
upon motives of more than common
enmity to Lord Granby, if I continued to
give you frefh materials or occafion for
writing in his defence. Individuals who
hate, and the public who defpife, have read
your letters, Sir William, with infinitely
more fatisfaction than mine. Unfortunately
for

for him, his reputation, like. that unhappy country to which you refer me for his last military, atchievements, has suffered more by his friends than his enemies.. In mercy to him, let us drop, the subject. For my own part, I willingly leave it to the public to determine whether your vindication of your friend has been as able and judicious, as it was certainly well, intended ; and you, I think, may be satisfied with the warm acknowledgements he. already owes you, for making him the principal figure in a piece, in which, but for your amicable affistance, he might have paffed without particular notice or diftinction.

In juftice to your friends, let your future labours be confined to the care of your own reputation. Your declaration, that you are happy in feeing young noblemen *come among us*, is liable to two objections. With refpect to Lord Percy, it means nothing, for he was already in the army. He was aid de camp to the King, and had the rank of colonel. A regiment therefore could not make him a more military man, though it made him richer, and probably at the expence of fome brave, deferving, friendlefs officer.—The other concerns yourfelf. After felling the companions of your victory in one inftance, and after felling your profeffion in the other,

by

by what authority do you prefume to call yourfelf a foldier ? The plain evidence of facts is
fuperior to all declarations. Before you were
appointed to the 16th regiment, your complaints were a diftrefs to government;—from
that moment you were filent. The conclufion is inevitable. You infinuate to us that
your ill ftate of health obliged you to quit the
fervice. The retirement neceffary to repair a
broken conftitution would have been as good
a reafon for not accepting, as for refigning
the command of a regiment. There is certainly an error of the prefs, or an affected
obfcurity in that paragraph, where you fpeak
of your bargain with colonel Gifborne. Inftead of attempting to anfwer what I do not
really underftand, permit me to explain to
the public what I really know. In exchange
for your regiment, you accepted of a colonel's
half-pay (at leaft 220l. a year) and an annuity of 200l. for your own and lady Draper's life jointly.—And is this the lofing
bargain, which you would reprefent to us, as
if you had given up an income of 800l. a
year for 380l. ? Was it decent, was it honourable, in a man, who pretends to love the
army, and calls himfelf a foldier, to make a
traffic of the royal favour, and turn the higheft honour of an active profeffion into a
fordid provifion for himfelf and his family?
It were unworthy of me to prefs you farther.

The

The contempt with which the whole army heard of the manner of your retreat, assures me, that as your conduct was not justified by precedent, it will never be thought an example for imitation.

THE last and most important question remains. When you receive your half-pay, do you, or do you not, take a solemn oath, or sign a declaration upon your honour, to the following effect? *That you do not actually hold any place of profit, civil or military, under his Majesty.* The charge which the question plainly conveys against you, is of so shocking a complection, that I sincerely wish you may be able to answer it well, not merely for the colour of your reputation, but for your own inward peace of mind.

J U N I U S.

L E T T E R VI.

TO JUNIUS.

SIR,   27 *February,* 1769.

I HAVE a very short answer for Junius's important question: I do not either take an oath, or declare upon honour, that I have no *place* of profit, *civil* or military,

when

when I receive the half-pay as an Irish colonel. My moft gracious Sovereign gives it me as a penfion: he was pleafed to think I deferved it. The annuity of 200l. Irifh, and the equivalent for the half-pay together, produces no more than 380l. per annum, clear of fees and perquifites of office. I receive 167l. from my government of Yarmouth. Total 547l. per annum. My confcience is much at eafe in thefe particulars,; my friends need not blufh for me.

JUNIUS makes much and frequent ufe of interrogations: they are arms that may be eafily turned againft himfelf. I could, by malicious interrogation, difturb the peace of the moft virtuous man in the kingdom; I could take the decalogue, and fay to one man, Did you never fteal? To the next, Did you never commit \murder? And to Junius himfelf, who is putting my life and conduct to the rack, Did you never bear falfe witnefs againft thy neighbour? Junius muft eafily fee, that unlefs he affirms to the contrary in his real name, fome people who may be as ignorant of him as I am, will be apt to fufpect him of having deviated a little from the truth: therefore let Junius afk no more queftions. You bite againft a file: ceafe, viper.

LET-

LETTER VII.

TO SIR WILLIAM DRAPER, KNIGHT OF
THE BATH.

SIR,   3 *March*, 1769.

AN academical education has given you
an unlimited command over the moſt
beautiful figures of ſpeech. Maſks, hatchets,
racks, and vipers dance through your letters in all the mazes of metaphorical confuſion. Theſe are the gloomy companions
of a diſturbed imagination ; the melancholy
madneſs of poetry, without the inſpiration.
I will not contend with you in point of
compoſition. You are a ſcholar, Sir William, and if I am truly informed, you write
Latin with almoſt as much purity as Engliſh.
Suffer me then, for I am a plain unlettered
man, to continue that ſtile of interrogation,
which ſuits my capacity, and to which, conſidering the readineſs of your anſwers, you
ought to have no objection. Even * Mr.

---

* BINGLEY was committed by the King's Bench for a
contempt of court, on which he made a voluntary oath,
that he would not anſwer interrogatories, unleſs he was
put to the torture.

Bingley

Bingley promises to anfwer, if put to the torture.

Do you then really think that, if I were to afk a *moft virtuous man* whether he ever committed theft, or murder, it would difturb his peace of mind ? Such a queftion might perhaps difcompofe the gravity of his mufcles, but I believe it would little affect the tranquility of his confcience. Examine your own breaft, Sir William, and you will difcover, that reproaches and enquiries have no power to afflict either the man of un-blemifhed integrity, or the abandoned profligate. It is the middle compound character which alone is vulnerable : the man, who, without firmnefs enough to avoid a difho-nourable action, has feeling enough to be afhamed of it.

I THANK you for the hint of the decalogue, and fhall take an opportunity of applying it to fome of your moft virtuous friends in both houfes of parliament.

You feem to have dropped the affair of your regiment ; fo let it reft. When you are appointed to another, I dare fay you will not fell it either for a grofs fum or for an annuity upon lives.

I AM truly glad (for really, Sir William, I am not your enemy, nor did I begin this conteft with you) that you have been able to clear yourfelf of a crime, though at the expence of the higheft indifcretion. You fay that your half-pay was given you by way of penfion. I will not dwell upon the fingularity of uniting in your own perfon two forts of provifion, which in their own nature, and in all military and parliamentary views, are incompatible ; but I call upon you to juftify that declaration, wherein you charge your Sovereign with having done an act in your favour notorioufly againft law. The half-pay, both in Ireland and England, is appropriated by parliament ; and if it be given to perfons, who, like you, are legally incapable of holding it, it is a breach of law. It would have been more decent in you to have called this difhonourable tranfaction by its true name ; a job to accommodate two perfons, by particular intereft and management at the caftle. What fenfe muft government have had of your fervices, when the rewards they have given you are only a difgrace to you !

AND now, Sir William, I fhall take my leave of you for ever. Motives very different from any apprehenfion of your refentment, make it impoffible you fhould ever

know

know me. In truth, you have fome reafon to hold yourfelf indebted to me. From the leffons I have given you, you may collect a profitable inftruction for your future life. They will either teach you fo to regulate your conduct, as to be able to fet the moft malicious inquiries at defiance; or, if that be a loft hope, they will teach you prudence enough not to attract the public attention to a character, which will only pafs without cenfure, when it paffes without obferva-tion*.

* SIR WILLIAM DRAPER's interference occafioned the Marquis of Granby's character to be more enlarged upon than was at firft intended. The conteft, for the prefent, clofed with this letter, the Marquis having fignified to Sir William to defift writing in his de-fence. On Wednefday the 17th of January 1770, the Marquis refigned all his places, except the Blues, and condemned openly in the Houfe of Commons that political fyftem, which had drawn on him the notice of Junius. He died in October, the fame year, univer-fally lamented.

LETTER

LETTER VIII.

TO THE DUKE OF GRAFTON.

MY LORD, 18 *March*, 1769.

BEFORE you were placed at the head of affairs, it had been a maxim of the Englifh government, not unwillingly admitted by the people, that every ungracious or fevere exertion of the prerogative fhould be placed to the account of the Minifter; but that, whenever an act of grace or benevolence was to be performed, the whole merit of it fhould be attributed to the Sovereign himfelf. It was a wife doctrine, my Lord, and equally advantageous to the 'King and his fubjects; for while it preferved that fufpicious attention with which the people ought always to examine the conduct of minifters, it tended at the fame time rather to increafe than diminifh their attachment to the perfon of their Sovereign. If there be not a fatality attending every meafure you are concerned in, by what treachery, or by what excefs of folly has it happened, that thofe ungracious acts, which have diftinguifhed your adminiftration, and which I doubt not were entirely your own, fhould carry with them a ftrong
appear-

appearance of perfonal intereft, and even of
perfonal enmity in a quarter, where no fuch
intereft or enmity can be fuppofed to exift,
without the higheft injuftice and the higheft
difhonour? On the other hand, by what
judicious management have you contrived
it, that the only act of mercy, to which
you ever advifed your Sovereign, far from
adding to the luftre of a character, truly
gracious and benevolent, fhould be received
with univerfal difapprobation and difguft?
I fhall confider it as a minifterial meafure,
becaufe it is an odious one, and as your meafure, my Lord Duke, becaufe you are the
minifter.

As long as the trial of this chairman was
depending, it was natural enough that government fhould give him every poffible en-
couragement and fupport. The honourable
fervice for which he was hired, and the fpirit
with which he performed it, made common
caufe between your grace and him. The
minifter, who by fecret corruption invades
the freedom of elections, and the ruffian,
who by open violence deftroys that freedom,
are embarked in the fame bottom. They
have the fame interefts, and mutually feel
for each other. To do juftice to your
Grace's humanity, you felt for MacQuirk
as you ought to do, and if you had been

con--

contented to affift him indirectly, without a
notorious denial of juftice, or openly infulting the fenfe of the nation, you might have
fatisfied every duty of political friendfhip,
without committing the honour of your Sovereign, or hazarding the reputation of his
government.   But when this unhappy man
had been folemnly tried, convicted and condemned; — when it appeared that he had
been frequently employed in the fame fervices, and that no excufe for him could be
drawn either from the innocence of his former
life, or the fimplicity of his character, was it
not hazarding too much to interpofe the
ftrength of the prerogative between this felon
and the juftice of his country* ?   You ought
to

* *Whitehall, March* 11, 1769. His Majefty has been
gracioufly pleafed to extend his royal mercy to Edward
M'Quirk, found guilty of the murder of George Clarke,
as appears by his royal warrant to the tenor following.

GEORGE R.

WHEREAS a doubt had arifen in Our Royal breaft
concerning the evidence of the death of George Clarke,
from the reprefentations of William Bromfield, Efq; Surgeon, and Solomon Starling, Apothecary; bothof whom,
as has been reprefented to Us, attended the deceafed before his death, and expreffed their opinions that he did
not die of the blow he received at Brentford : And
whereas it appears to Us, that neither of the faid perfons
were produced as witneffes upon the trial, though the
faid

to have known that an example of this fort
was never fo neceffary as at prefent; and
certainly you muft have known that the lot
could not have fallen upon a more guilty
D 4   objeét.

faid Solomon Starling had been examined before the
Coroner, and the only perfon called to prove that the
death of the faid George Clarke was occafioned by the
faid blow, was John Foot, Surgeon, who never faw the
deceafed till after his death ; We thought fit thereupon
to refer the faid reprefentations, together with the report
of the Recorder of Our city of London, of the evidence
given by Richard and William Beale, and the faid John
Foot, on the trial of Edward Quirk, otherwife called
Edward Kirk, otherwife called Edward M'Quirk, for the
murder of the faid Clark, to the mafter, wardens, and the
reft of the court of examiners of the Surgeons company,
commanding them likewife to take fuch further exami-
nation of the faid perfons fo reprefenting, and of faid
John Foot, as they might think neceffary, together with
the premifes abovementioned, to form and report to Us
their opinion, " Whether it did or did not appear to
" them, that the faid George Clarke died in confequence
" of the blow he received in the riot at Brentford on
" the 8th of December laft." And the faid court of
examiners of the Surgeons company having thereupon
reported to Us their opinion, " That it did not appear to
" them that he did ;" We have thought proper to extend
Our royal mercy to him the faid Edward Quirk, otherwife
called Edward Kirk, otherwife called Edward M'Quirk,
and to grant him our free pardon for the Murder of the
faid George Clarke, of which he has been found guilty :
Our will and pleafure therefore is, That he the faid
Edward Quirk, otherwife called Edward Kirk, otherwife
called Edward M'Quirk, be inferted, for the faid Murder

object. What system of government is this ?
You are perpetually complaining of the riot-
ous disposition of the lower class of people,
yet when the laws have given you the means
of making an example, in every sense unexceptionable, and by far the most likely to
awe the multitude, you pardon the offence,
and are not ashamed to give the sanction of
government to the riots you complain of, and
even to future murders. You are partial
perhaps to the military mode of execution,
and had rather see a score of these wretches
butchered by the guards, than one of them
suffer death by regular course of law. How
does it happen, my Lord, that in *your* hands,
even the mercy of the prerogative is cruelty
and oppression to the subject ?

der, in Our first and next general pardon that shall come
out for the poor convicts of Newgate, without any condition whatsoever ; and that in the mean time you take
bail for his appearance, in order to plead Our said pardon. And for so doing this shall be your warrant.

> Given at Our court at St. James's the 10th day of
> March, 1769, in the ninth year of Our reign.
> By his Majesty's command,
>   ROCHFORD.

To our trusty and well beloved James
Eyre, Esq; Recorder of Our city of
London, the Sheriffs of Our said
city and county of Middlesex, and
all others whom it may concern.

THE

THE meafure it feems was fo extraordinary, that you thought it neceffary to give fome reafons for it to the public. Let them be fairly examined.

1. You fay *that Meffrs: Bromfield and Starling were not examined at MacQuirk's trial.* I will tell your Grace why they were not. They muft have been examined upon oath; and it was forefeen, that their evidence would either not benefit, or might be prejudicial to the prifoner. Otherwife, is it conceivable that his counfel fhould neglect to call in fuch material evidence.

You fay that *Mr: Foot did not fee the deceafed until after his death.* A furgeon, my Lord, muft know very little of his profeffion, if, upon examining a wound, or a contufion, he cannot determine whether it was mortal or not.—While the party is alive, a furgeon will be cautious of pronouncing; whereas by the death of the patient, he is enabled to confider both caufe and effect in one view, and to fpeak with a certainty confirmed by experience.

YET we are to thank your Grace for the eftablifhment of a new tribunal. Your *inquifitio poft mortem* is unknown to the laws of England, and does honour to your invention.

The

The only material objection to it is, that if
Mr. Foot's evidence was infufficient, becaufe
he did not examine the wound till after the
death of the party, much lefs can a negative
opinion, given by gentlemen who never faw
the body of Mr. Clarke, either before or after his deceafe, authorife you to fuperfede
the verdict of a jury, and the fentence of the
law.

Now, my Lord, let me afk you, Has it
never occurred to your Grace, while you
were withdrawing this defperate wretch from
that juftice which the laws had awarded,
and which the whole people of England demanded againft him, that there is another
man, who is the favourite of his country,
whofe pardon would have been accepted with
gratitude, whofe pardon would have healed
all our divifions? Have you quite forgotten
that this man was once your Grace's friend?
Or is it to murderers only that you will extend the mercy of the crown.

THESE are queftions you will not anfwer.
Nor is it neceffary. The character of your
private life, and the uniform tenour of your
public conduct, is an anfwer to them all.

J U N I U S.

LETTER IX.

A VINDICATION OF THE DUKE OF
GRAFTON, IN ANSWER TO A LETTER
SIGNED JUNIUS.

THE foregoing letter of Junius addreſſed
to the Duke of Grafton, produced a
vindication of his Grace in a pamphlet of
forty-ſeven pages, by one who calls himſelf,
A Volunteer in the Service of Government, and
takes God to witneſs that neither his Grace,
nor any other ſervant of the crown has the
leaſt intimation or knowledge of it. This
gentleman has entered fully into the merits
of the complaint; and has, he thinks, ex-
poſed the wit, ſophiſtry, and malice of Junius, with common ſenſe, truth, and good
nature.

THE maxim, he ſays, of Engliſh government, (that the king can do no wrong) of
which Junius endeavours to pervert the ſenſe,
owes its birth to a cataſtrophe, and is adopted as a bar againſt a like event on a like occaſion. But to ſay that every ungracious
and ſevere exertion of the prerogative is to be
placed to the account of the miniſter; and
every act of grace and benevolence to that of

D 6   the

the king, as Junius hath advanced, is as falfe
as unjuft ; for it is as much the duty of a minifter to advife in the latter cafe as in the
former ; and he is therefore entitled to fhare
in the praife that may refult from the one, full
as much as in the blame that may be laid on
the other.

THE ungracious acts of his Grace's adminiftration, alluded to by Junius, the Volunteer, fuppofes are :

1. THAT fole mitigated act of juftice
which the firft and moft infolent of all offenders of his clafs has drawn upon himfelf,
and,

2. THAT act of mercy which Junius has
made the fubject of his abufe.

As to the appearance of perfonal intereft
and perfonal enmity operating, in the firft
cafe, from a quarter where no fuch intereft or
enmity can be fuppofed to exift ; fhould it
be true, that the criminal has offended that
quarter by the vileft afperfions in the moft
tender point, a point too facred to be recollected, and which no nation on earth, except our own, would have borne to be attempted ; that to this purpofe he had amufed,
inflamed, and bewitched the minds of the
young

young and lively, by the moft villainous and
moft infernal inuendos, ftri&ures, and in-
terpretations, on an intercourfe which had
been folely founded on the moft cogent and
moft virtuous motives; under fuch unme-
rited and unparalleled provocation, kings
muft either be fuppofed to be Gods or Brutes
not to be fufceptible of the deepeft impref-
fions.

In the fecond cafe, it muft have occurred
to his Grace, that the latter was an honeft
fellow in comparifon to the former. That
he was a low-bred, ill-advifed, unhappy
wretch, who, from being employed by his
betters, in feveral contefted ele&ions, to a&
according to their occafional commands, with
the utmoft impunity, had taken it for granted, that the licentioufnefs of an ele&ion riot
was beyond the reach of the laws. That,
having been intoxicated with liquor, or deceived by a filly or malicious prompter, or
fignal, he fancied himfelf to be called upon,
to drive the adverfary from the field of conteft.
That he was but one, of many, who had been
led, or had fallen into the fame error with himfelf, and who, by laying about them like mad-
men, committed more mifchief than they ever
intended ; efpecially, by ftriking an unlucky
blow, of which the perfon who received it
was afferted to have died ; and whofe death,
by

by the coroner's inqueſt, was deemed wilful
murder by a perſon or perſons unknown.
That, notwithſtanding this verdict, the ſur-
geon who had attended him before he died,
had informed the Secretary of State, that he
was of a very different opinion. That, more-
over, the culprit was ſo little aware of having
had any ſhare in that particular accident; and
was ſo little aprehenſive of reſearches to be
made after the individuals of an election riot,
that he had not only returned to the buſineſs
of his legal calling, but had had the imprudence to converſe on what he had done, with
his friends and acquaintance. That having
met with a perſon, who by his birth and appearance was a gentleman, and whom he
had ſaved from a blow, which might have
proved as fatal as the other; he had not
ſcrupled to accept of his offer, of treating him
with ſome liquor by way of gratitude, nor of
relating to him whatever he knew of the riot,
and of his own ſhare in it. That he had been
ſhamefully betrayed by this pretended grateful gentleman. That he had no ſooner been
made ſenſible, by his impending fate, of the
unlawfulneſs and criminality of this election
buſineſs, but he had cried out for mercy, with
promiſes of never being guilty of the like
for the future. That he had not been indict-
ed, and condemned for murder, but for aid-
ing and abetting in it. That theſe and many

ny other circumftances did certainly plead in
his favour. But then, that his trial and con-
demnation had been attended with circumftances on the part of the audience, which had
fhocked all decency and humanity; and had
fhown, at the fame time, fuch a fpirit of refentment and infatuation in thofe who had
been the opponents of the candidate, whofe
fuccefs he had fpoiled by his mifconduct, as
was highly and criminally reflecting on government, as if the execution of this convict
was to have been a mere facrifice to liberty,
falfely pretended to be injured by government itfelf. That this latter was a nettling
occurrence. That it was as dangerous for
the miniftry to abandon this poor fellow to
the feverity of the law, as to give way to the
circumftances which pleaded for his pardon.
That if he was hanged, the crafty difturbers
of public tranquility would not fail to fay, that
the miniftry had been afraid to lay his cafe
before the King; and had facrificed the poor
fellow, to their fear of fhewing him to be
their own tool, by recommending him to the
royal mercy. That if, on the other hand,
they complied with the duties of their fta-
tions, in laying before the King, the inter-
ceffions that were made in his behalf, with
the circumftances upon which they were
founded; the fame revilers of government
would not fail to fay, in cafe his Majefty
fhould

should grant his pardon, that this royal act
was a contrivance of their own, to save their
tool from the gallows, and to bind him thereby to secrecy. That, in good policy, the latter was, however, preferable to the other.
That if the man was hanged, the rascals could
make him a dying speech of their own invention, pretending it to have been conveyed to them one way or other. That, on the
contrary, if he was kept alive, and set at liberty, it would not be so easy for them to
engage a man, who had once escaped so nar-
rowly the power of the law, to stand the
chance of being tried for perjury. But after
all, that honesty was the best policy, and that
therefore, the most eligible of all was, to pay
no attention to whatever the malice of others,
or one's own interest might suggest, but to
keep up to the rules of office, as well as to
those of justice and humanity; to let the applications for mercy take their natural course
to the throne, full as much as those for justice
had done to the bar; to let the circumstances alledged be referred to whatever
persons, courts, or offices, were entitled to
report on the same, and to let his Majesty
determine from thence, according to the
dictates of his own wisdom, justice, and
clemency.

I SHALL

I SHALL, therefore, fays this Volunteer, leave it to the public to judge, whether they ought not to defpife, and even to deteft- and abhor the fafcinating powers of Junius's infernal pen ; and not fuffer themfelves to be attracted by the deceitful colour and flavour of the moft fubtle and penetrating poifon that ever was invented, except by that arch fiend of his king and country, to whofe fociety, and his fociety alone, Junius deferves to be confined for ever, by fuch a punifhment as in juftice and good policy, if not in law, ought to be inflicted on every man, whofe powerful talents, of what nature foever, are only employed to the deftruction of civil fociety, and fubverfion of a ftate.

WITH refpect to Mr. Wilkes, the Volunteer acknowledges, that the Duke was one of his betters, that had once been his friend ; that he had not·fcrupled when Secretary of State to join his purfe to thofe of others to maintain the culprit in his own expenfive way, whilft he was confidered as an outlaw ; but that being at laft convinced of the apparent refolution of this defperate criminal, to attempt as far as he could the ruin of his country, in order to gratify his own extravagant prodigality and Catalinian ambition, he had refolved, in his turn, not only totally to abandon him to the perverfity of his na-

ture

ture, and to the tremendous confequences of
his defperate conduct, but to act the part of
a moft zealous and moft faithful fervant of
the crown, of one of the guardians of the
conftitution, and of one of the reftorers of
the public tranquility, to the terror and deftruction of this and every other feditious
firebrand, who fhould continue to pervert
and inflame the minds of his Majefty's unguarded fubjects.

LETTER X.

TO HIS GRACE THE DUKE OF GRAFTON.

MY LORD,   10 *April*, 1769.

I HAVE fo good an opinion of your
Grace's difcernment, that when the author of the vindication of your conduct affures us, that he writes from his own mere
motion, without the leaft authority from
your Grace, I fhould be ready enough to believe him, but for one fatal mark, which
feems to be fixed upon every meafure, in
which either your perfonal or your political
character is concerned.—Your firft attempt
to fupport Sir William Proctor ended in the
election of Mr. Wilkes; the fecond enfured
fuccefs to Mr. Glynn. The extraordinary
                                        ftep

ftep you took to make Sir James Lowther
Lord Paramount of Cumberland, has ruined
his intereft in that county for ever. The
Houfe Lift of Directors was curfed with the
concurrence of government; and even the
miferable * Dingley could not efcape the
misfortune of your Grace's protection. With
this uniform experience before us, we are
authorifed to fufpect, that when a pretended
vindication of your principles and conduct
in reality contains the bittereft reflections
upon both, it could not have been written
without your immediate direction and affiftance. The author indeed calls God to witnefs for him, with all the fincerity, and in
the very terms of an Irifh evidence, *to the beft
of his knowledge and belief*. My Lord, you
fhould not encourage thefe appeals to heaven.
The pious Prince, from whom you are fuppofed to defcend, made fuch frequent ufe of
them in his public declarations, that at laft
the people alfo found it neceffary to appeal to
heaven in their turn. Your adminiftration
has driven us into circumftances of equal
diftrefs;—beware at leaft how you remind
us of the remedy.

* Mr. Dingley was perfuaded by the Duke to ftand
candidate for Middlefex, but he could not prevail on any
freeholder to put him in nomination.

You

You have already much to anfwer for.
You have provoked this unhappy gentleman
to play the fool once more in public life, in
fpite of his years and infirmities, and to fhew
us, that, as you yourfelf are a fingular-in-
ftance of youth without fpirit, the man who
defends you is a no lefs remarkable example
of age without the benefits of experience.
To follow fuch a writer minutely would,
like his own periods, be a labour without
end. The fubject too has been already difcuffed, and is fufficiently underftood. I cannot help obferving, however, that, when the
pardon of MacQuirk was the principal
charge againft you, it would have been but
a decent compliment to your Grace's underftanding, to have defended you upon your
own principles. What credit does a man deferve, who tells us plainly, that the facts fet
forth in the King's proclamation were not
the true motives on which the pardon was
granted, and that he wifhes that thofe chirurgical reports, which firft gave occafion to
certain doubts in the royal breaft, had not
been laid before his Majefty. You fee, my
Lord, that even your friends cannot defend
your actions, without changing your principles, nor juftify a deliberate meafure of
government, without contradicting the main
affertion on which it was founded.

THE

THE conviction of MacQuirk had reduced you to a dilemma, in which it was hardly poſſible for you to reconcile your political
intereſt with your duty. You were obliged
either to abandon an active uſeful partiſan,
or to protect a felon from public juſtice.
With your uſual ſpirit, you preferred your
intereſt to every other conſideration ; and
with your uſual judgment, you founded
your determination upon the only motives,
which ſhould not have been given to the
public. .

I HAVE frequently cenſured Mr. Wilkes's
conduct, yet your advocate reproaches me
with having devoted myſelf to the ſervice
of ſedition. Your Grace can beſt inform
us, for which of Mr. Wilkes's good qualities
you firſt honoured him with your friendſhip,
or how long it was before you diſcovered
thoſe bad ones in him, at which, it ſeems,
your delicacy was offended. Remember, my
Lord, that you continued your connexion
with Mr. Wilkes long after he had been convicted of thoſe crimes, which you have ſince
taken pains to repreſent in the blackeſt colours of blaſphemy and treaſon. How unlucky is it, that the firſt inſtance you have
given us of a ſcrupulous regard to decorum is
united with the breach of a moral obligation !
For my own part, my Lord, I am proud to
affirm,

affirm, that, if I had been weak enough to form such a friendſhip, I would never have been baſe enough to betray it. But, let Mr. Wilkes's character be what it may, this at leaſt is certain, that, circumſtanced as he is with regard to the public, even his vices plead for him. The people of England have too much diſcernment to ſuffer your Grace to take advantage of the failings of a private character, to eſtabliſh a precedent by which the public liberty is affected, and which you may hereafter, with equal eaſe and ſatisfaction, employ to the ruin of the beſt men in the kingdom. ——Content yourſelf, my Lord, with the many advantages, which the unſullied purity of your own character has given you over your unhappy deſerted friend. Avail yourſelf of all the unforgiving piety of the court you live in, and bleſs God that you " are not as " other men are ; extortioners, unjuſt, adul- " terers, or even as this publican." In a heart void of feeling, the laws of honour and good faith may be violated with impunity, and there you may ſafely indulge your genius. But the laws of England ſhall not be violated, even by your holy zeal to oppreſs a ſinner ; and though you have ſucceeded in making him a tool, you ſhall not make him the victim of your ambition.

JUNIUS.
LETTER

LETTER XI.

REPLY TO THE ABOVE LETTER BY THE VOLUNTEER.

SHOULD I be fo unlucky, fays he, not to have defended your Grace on your own principles, it fhould not be for mine, but for your own, and the public's fake, that I fhould be forry. But this pretenfion of Mafter Junius is too fallacious to be dwelt upon ; and I fhall truft to the fteadinefs of your Grace's public conduct to give him the lie in this refpect. In the mean while I fhall do fo here, in vindication of my own veracity, and to clear myfelf of his falfe and impudent affertion of my having told plainly, " that the facts fet forth in the king's proclamation were not the true motives on which the pardon was granted." To fay that I have directly or indirectly told this, is as grofs a lie as he or any man ever uttered. I have indeed told the public, and I repeat it here, that I could not but regret that the Earl of Rochford, whether with, or without the concurrence of his co-minifters, feemed to have thought proper to lay the chirurgical reports before the king in preference to all the other fufficient motives that were alledged,

and

and were, or might have been fuggefted to
his majefty in behalf of the pardoned convict.
But this implies in the fulleft manner, that
the pardon was granted by the king, in confequence of thofe reports, as it was fet forth
in the proclamation. And as to the confequence which Junius draws from his lie, the
latter part vanifhes with it, and the other
fhews him to be as void of logic as of truth;
for what has the mode of an action to do
with its principle. I fuppofe for a moment
that your Grace had a mind, from a due regard to juftice and the public fafety, to get
this Junius punifhed according to his defert, would it change your principle, whether you thought proper to have it done by
a horfe-whip, by an axe, or by an halter?
No more, I hope, my Lord Duke, could it
change the principle of juftice and humanity, on which you advifed the pardon of
M'Quirk, whether it was done with laying
before the king any other circumftance which
pleaded in his favour, or that of the chirurgical opinions and reports.

LETTER XII.

TO MR. EDWARD WESTON.*

S I R, 21 *April*, 1769.

I SAID you were an old man without the benefit of experience. It feems you are alfo a volunteer with the ftipend of twenty commiffions ; and at a period when all profpeds are at an end, you are ftill looking forward to rewards, which you cannot enjoy. No man is better acquainted with the bounty of government than you are,

——*ton impudence,*
Temeraire vieillard, aura fa recompenfe.

---

* A privy counfellor in Ireland, writer of the Gazette, comptroller of the falt office, one of the chief clerks of the fignet, and a penfioner on the Irifh eftablifhment. A charge was brought againft him in the news papers, that when he was under Secretary of State, the divifion of 500l. among ten people was left to his difcretion, 400l. of which he modeftly claimed for his own fhare. Such is this volunteer ! the volunteer, to this charge, confeffes that he knows Mr. Wefton, but declares upon his honour, that the Right Hon. Mr. Wefton has never had the leaft fhare in, or knowledge of this vindication of the Duke of Grafton ; and as to his claim of 400l. out of 500l. he is fure it muft be a downright lie, or a grofs mifreprefentation.

VOL. I. E BUT

BUT I will not defcend to an altercation either with the impotence of your age, or the peevifhnefs of your difeafes. Your pamphlet, ingenious as it is, has been fo little read, that the public cannot know how far you have a right to give me the lye, without the following citation of your own words.

Page 6—' 1. That he is perfuaded that ' the motives, which he (Mr. Wefton) has ' alledged, muft appear fully fufficient, with ' or without the opinions of the furgeons.

' THAT thofe very motives MUST HAVE ', BEEN the foundation, on which the Earl of ' Rochford thought proper, &c.

' THAT he CANNOT BUT REGRET that ' the Earl of Rochford feems to have thought ' proper to lay the chirurgical reports before ' the king, in preference to all the other fuf- ' ficient motives,' &c.

LET the public determine whether this be defending government on their principles or your own.

THE ftyle and language you have adopted are, I confefs, not ill fuited to the elegance of your own manners, or to the dignity of the caufe you have undertaken. Every common
                                                    dauber

dauber writes rafcal and villain under his pictures, becaufe the pictures themfelves have neither character nor refemblance. But the works of a mafter require no index. His features and colouring are taken from nature. The impreflion they make is immediate and uniform ; nor is it poffible to miftake his characters, whether they reprefent the treachery of a minifter, or the abufed fimplicity of a ——*.

J U N I U S.

A M O N O D Y. XIII.

OR THE TEARS OF SEDITION ON THE DEATH OF JUNIUS.

Quis tibi Silure furor ?

AND are thofe periods fill'd with tuneful
  care,
 Thofe thoughts which gleam'd with Cice-
  ronian ore,
Are they, my Junius, pafs'd like vulgar air,
 Droop'd is thy plume, to rife on fame no
  more ?

Thy plume !—it was the harp of fong in profe :
 Oft have its numbers footh'd the felon's ear,

---

* The word " *king*" was left blank in the original publication.

Oft

Oft to it's tune my Wilkite heroes rofe
　With couch'd tobacco pipes in act to fpear.

Where now fhall ftormy Clodius and his crew,
　My dear affembly to the midnight hour,
Ah! where acquire a trumpeter?—fince you
　No more fhall rouze them with your claffic
　　power.

Accurs'd * Silerus! blafted be thy wing!
　That grey Scotch wing which led th' uner-
　　ring dart!
In virtue's caufe could all that's fatire fting
　A bofom with corruption's poifon fraught!

Impoffible!—then hear me, fiends of Hell,
　This dark event, this myftery unfold;
Poifon'd was Junius? No; " Alas, he fell,
　" 'Midft arrows dipp'd in minifterial gold."

Then hear me, rioters, of my command,
　Condemn the villain to a traitor's doom;
Let none but faithful knaves adorn my band;
　Go, fink this character into his tomb.

Here funk an effayift of dubious name,
　Whofe tinfel'd page on airy cadence run,
Friendlefs, with party—noted without fame,
　Virtue and vice difclaim'd him as a fon.
　　　　　　　　POETICASTOS.

　　* A writer in oppofition to Wilkes.
　　　　　　　　　　　　　This

This little piece produced the following re-- markable explanations.

L E T T.E R XIV.

TO POETICASTOS.

THE Monody on the fuppofed death of Junius is not lefs poetical for being founded on a fiction. In fome parts of it, there is a promife of genius, which deferves to be encouraged. My letter of Monday [April 10,] will, I hope, convince the author that I am neither a partizan of Mr. Wilkes, nor yet bought off by the miniftry. It is true I have refufed offers, which a more prudent or a more interefted man would have accepted. Whether it be fimplicity or virtue in me, I can only affirm that I am in earneft; becaufe I am convinced, as far as my underftanding is capable of judging, that the prefent miniftry is driving this country to deftruction; and you, I think Sir, may be fatisfied that my rank and fortune place me above a common bribe.

J U N I U S.

A CARD. XV.

TO JUNIUS.

POETICASTOS prefents his compli-
ments to Junius, and is glad to underftand from fo celebrated a judge of the beautiful and fublime, that there is " a promife of
genius" in his Monody. He could wifh
that it were in his power, either as a man of
tafte or honour, to pay Junius any return of
praife : as the motive and manner of the Effayift deprive Poeticaftos of this power, he muft
take the liberty of cautioning him never to
expofe himfelf fo far again, as to make a line
of doggrel the fuppofed caufe of announcing
his fictitious importance to the public. .

IF Junius dares to be fincere, inftead of
being in earneft, let him point out the deftruction to which the minifters are driving
this country, in a more rational and gentle-
manlike manner than that ill-bred and cow-
ardly method in which he would ftain the
perfonal honour of the minifter, without
being able to detract from the propriety of his
meafures.

LET him not hint at the offers which he
had not the prudence to accept,—let him
publifh

publifh them particularly and exprefsly. Let him not afk for an uncommon bribe on account of a fuppofed rank and fortune, or affert, in childifh terms, that he is not a partifan of Mr. Wilkes, but let the fpirit of his writing fhew, that he is neither a hungry traducer of the merits of character, nor the hireling of the moft contemptible of parties.

POETICASTOS will then, and not till then, have fo favourable an idea of Junius, as to give him fome credit—he will perhaps offer him fome more poetical compofitions, and be defirous of a perfonal acquaintance with a reformed or undeceived imitator of a TULLY.

L E T T E R XVI.

TO JUNIUS.

I ALWAYS fufpected your honefty. You have now convinced me of your cowardice. Unable and afraid to anfwer a charge of difhonour brought publicly againft you in the language of refolution, you now begin to crow over the infirmities of a man confeffedly incapable of chaftifing your infolence in any refpect. Is, Sir, the public to be abufed any longer with your fcandalous im-

pofi-

pofitions? Or how dare you to pretend, after fwallowing a lye like a fcoundrel, to appear again before the world, as if you could merit attention? But you would offer the judgment of the nation a more glaring affront; you would give a bluftering air of refolution to the timid bafenefs of your heart, by daring to fpeak treafon in a manner that you are fure of efcaping. To day you conclude your defpicable vindication of an honour which you do not poffefs, by afferting " that you are a mafter in the art of reprefenting the treachery of the minifter, and the abufed fimplicity of a —————." Villain! of whom? Dare to fill the blank! but you fay it is unneceffary.—Every man in the kingdom underftands you. If they do, I appeal to them what punifhment you merit; and if the law will not inflict it, I will, if you have the fhadow of fenfibility. You who write under the name of Junius, are a bafe fcoundrel; you lye, and you may find out who gives you the lye. If you dare to appear in this paper again, without an apology for your conduct, I will convince you I am not ignorant of your perfon and refidence.

POETICASTOS.

To this feveral anfwers appeared, but the following bears the true fpirit of Junius.

LETTER

L E T T E R XVII.

TO POETICASTOS.

S I R,

POETICASTOS in his letter to Junius,
is in such a violent rage, that he forgets to sign his real name. The *blood and
thunder*, the *storming, ranting*, and *blustering*
in his short epistle could have come from
none but Drawcansir himself. He grows
raving mad at the following extract which he
quotes from Junius's letter, viz. that he is a
" master in the art of representing the trea-
" chery of the minister, and the abused
" simplicity of a —— ;" and then follows
the word villain, and in so ambiguous a
manner, that many readers are in doubt
whether it is not intended to fill up the ——,
and to prepare the challenge that follows.
Now, Sir, whether Drawcansir intended it
or not, or whether Junius will accept his
challenge or not, I am determined to meet
him whenever he chooses it; and if he is a
Scotchman, I will smother him in his own
brimstone; if a Welchman, hur shall eat hur
own leeks; if Irish, he shall chew potatoes
from the mouth of my pistol; and for this

E 5   infa-

infamous way of filling up the blanks in
Junius's letter, he fhall no longer fill another
blank in the creation.

HECTOR.

A C A R D XVIII.

POETICASTOS prefents his compli-
ments to the redoubtable fupporters of
the Bill of Rights, and returns them a thoufand thanks for the ufe which he had ventur-
ed to take of their new method of over-
coming enemies without fpilling of blood,
and of acquiring laurels without moving
from the tavern. He takes the liberty, as
they have given no name to that new engine
with which they have overfet the Coventry
addreffers, to beftow on it the title of the
Patriotic Blunderbufs, and fires it thus upon
his dreadful adverfary, Junius, Hector, and
Crito, in one perfon.

Bedlam, April 27, 1769.

Poeticaftos in his chair.

Refolved, That the Advifer, Author, and
Publifher of Junius's Letters are too contemptible to merit the further notice of his
pen.

By my own order,

Myfelf Secretary,   POETICASTOS.

LETTER

L E T T E R XIX.

TO HIS GRACE THE DUKE OF GRAFTON.

MY LORD,   24 *April*, 1769.

THE fyftem you feem to have adopted, when Lord Chatham unexpectedly left you at the head of affairs, gave us no promife of that uncommon exertion of vigour, which has fince illuftrated your character, and diftinguifhed your adminiftration. Far from difcovering a fpirit bold enough to invade the firft rights of the people, and the firft principles of the conftitution, you were fcrupulous of exercifing even thofe powers, with which the executive branch of the legiflature is legally invefted. We have not yet forgotten how long Mr. Wilkes was fuffered to appear at large, nor how long he was at liberty to canvafs for the city and couhty, with all the terrors of an outlawry hanging over him. Our gracious Sovereign has not yet forgotten the extraordinary care you took of his dignity and of the fafety of his perfon, when at a crifis which courtiers affected to call alarming, you left the metropolis expofed, for two nights together, to every fpecies of riot and diforder. The fecurity of the Royal refidence from

E 6   infult

insult was then sufficiently provided for in Mr. Conway's firmness, and Lord Weymouth's discretion; while the prime minister of Great Britain, in a rural retirement, and in the arms of faded beauty, had lost all memory of his Sovereign, his country and himself. In these instances you might have acted with vigour, for you would have had the sanction of the laws to support you. The friends of government might have defended you without shame, and moderate men, who wish well to the peace and good order of society, might have had a pretence for applauding your conduct. But these it seems were not occasions worthy of your Grace's interposition. You reserved the proofs of your intrepid spirit for trials of greater hazard and importance; and now, as if the most disgraceful relaxation of the executive authority had given you a claim of credit to indulge in excesses still more dangerous, you seem determined to compensate amply for your former negligence; and to balance the non-execution of the laws with a breach of the constitution. From one extreme you suddenly start to the other, without leaving, between the weakness and the fury of the passions, one moment's interval for the firmness of the understanding.

THESE

THESE observations, general as they are, might easily be extended into a faithful history of your Grace's administration, and perhaps may be the employment of a future hour. But the business of the present moment will not suffer me to look back to a series of events, which cease to be interesting or important, because they are succeeded by a measure so singularly daring, that it excites all our attention, and engrosses all our resentment.

YOUR patronage of Mr. Luttrell has been crowned with success. With this precedent before you, with the principles on which it was established, and with a future house of commons, perhaps less virtuous than the present, every county in England, under the auspices of the Treasury, may be represented as completely as the county of Middlesex. Posterity will be indebted to your Grace for not contenting yourself with a temporary expedient, but entailing upon them the immediate blessings of your administration. Boroughs were already too much at the mercy of government. Counties could neither be purchased nor intimidated. But their solemn determined election may be rejected, and the man they detest may be appointed, by another choice, to represent them in parliament. Yet it is admitted, that the sheriffs obeyed the laws

and

and performed their duty*. 'The return they made muſt have been legal and valid, or undoubtedly they would have been cenſured for making it. With every good-natured allowance for your Grace's youth and inexperience, there are ſome things which you cannot but know. You cannot but know that the right of the freeholders to adhere to their choice (even ſuppoſing it improperly exerted) was as clear and indiſputable as that of the houſe of commons to exclude one of their own members ?—nor is it poſſible for you not to ſee the wide diſtance there is between the negative power of rejecting one man, and the poſitive power of appointing another. The right of expulſion, in the moſt favourable ſenſe, is no more than the cuſtom of parliament. The right of election is the very eſſence of the conſtitution. To violate that right, and much more to transfer it to any other ſet of men, is a ſtep leading immediately to the diſſolution of all government. So far forth as it operates, it conſtitutes a houſe of commons, which *does not* repreſent the people. A houſe of commons ſo formed would involve a contradiction and the groſſeſt confuſion of ideas; but there are ſome miniſters, my Lord,

* EvEN Sir Fletcher Norton declared in the houſe of Commons, that the Sheriffs in returning Mr. Wilkes, had done no more than their duty.

whoſe

whofe views can only be anfwered by recon-
ciling abfurdities, and making the fame propofition, which is falfe and abfurd in argument, true in fact.

' THIS meafure, my Lord, is however attended with one confequence, favourable to
the people, which I am perfuaded you did not
forefee. While the conteft lay between the
miniftry and Mr. Wilkes, his fituation and
private character gave you advantages over
him, which common candour, if not the memory of your former friendfhip, fhould have
forbidden you to make ufe of. To religious
men, you had an opportunity of exaggerating
the irregularities of his paft life—to moderate men you held forth the pernicious confequences of faction. Men, who with this
character, looked no farther than to the object
before them, were not diffatisfied at feeing
Mr. Wilkes excluded from parliament. You
have now taken care to fhift the queftion; or,
rather, you have created a new one, in which
Mr. Wilkes is no more concerned than any
other Englifh gentleman. You have united
this country againft you on one grand conftitutional point, on the decifion of which our
exiftence, as a free people, abfolutely depends.
You have afferted, not in words but in fact,
that the reprefentation in parliament does not
depend upon the choice of the freeholders.

If

If such a case can possibly happen once, it may happen frequently ; it may happen always :—and if three hundred votes, by any mode of reasoning whatsoever, can prevail against twelve hundred, the same reasoning would equally have given Mr. Luttrell his seat with ten votes, or even with one. The consequences of this attack upon the constitution are too plain and palpable not to alarm the dullest apprehension. I trust you will find, that the people of England are neither deficient in spirit nor understanding, though you have treated them, as if they had neither sense to feel, nor spirit to resent. We have reason to thank God and our ancestors, that there never yet was a minister in this country, who could stand the issue of such a conflict ; and with every prejudice in favour of your intentions, I see no such abilities in your Grace, as should entitle you to succeed in an enterprize, in which the ablest and basest of your predecessors have found their destruction. You may continue to deceive your gracious master with false representations of the temper and condition of his subjects. You may command a venal vote, because it is the common established appendage of your office. But never hope that the freeholders will make a tame surrender of their rights, or that an English army will join with you in overturning the liberties of their country.

'They

They know that their firſt duty as citizens is paramount to all ſubſequent engagements, nor will they prefer the diſcipline or even the honours. of their profeſſion to thoſe ſacred original rights, which belonged to them before they were ſoldiers, and which they claim and poſſeſs as the birth-right of Engliſhmen.

RETURN, my Lord, before it be too late, to that eaſy inſipid ſyſtem, which you firſt ſet out with. Take back your miſtreſs; *——
the

* ANN PARSONS. When the Duke obtained a divórce from his Wife, he wrote his Miſtreſs the following letter:

MADAM,

ON the final difference I had with my lady, I connected myſelf with you, as one, I thought, whoſe perſonal and mental qualifications were ſuch, as would in a great meaſure alleviate my domeſtic misfortunes. My expectations, I muſt do you the juſtice to ſay, were perfectly anſwered; and it would be perhaps difficult even for ill-nature to point out a ſingle defect in your truth and unwearied aſſiduity to pleaſe me; but as I often told you (particularly at our firſt interview, that I ſhould have nothing in future to charge myſelf with) that ſuch a courſe of life was unſeemly both in my moral and political character, and that nothing but the neceſſity could juſtify the meaſure, I am now to tell you (that obſtacle being removed by the laws) that all our former ties are, from this day, at an end.

I HAVE

the name of friend may be fatal to her, for it leads to treachery and perfecution. Indulge the people. Attend Newmarket. Mr. Luttrell' may again vacate his feat; and Mr.

Wilkes

I HAVE taken care, my dear friend (for I will now totally throw by the lover) to make that eftablifhment for you, as will make you eafy in your circumftances for life, chargeable only with this provifo, that your refidence be not in thefe kingdoms; the reft of Europe lies at your choice; and you have only to fend me word on your arrival where you are, and the next poft fhall carry you your firft quarterly payment.

ASSURE yourfelf, that nothing fhould induce me to act in this manner, but the determined refolution I have taken, now that it is in my power, of fpeedily entering into chafter connections; and that I am, and ever fhall be, with great efteem and friendfhip,

Your's, &c.

THE ANSWER.

MY VERY DEAR LORD,

(FOR I will not—indeed I cannot—retaliate your coldnefs) nothing could have furprifed me more than your letter. It is very true you did infinuate on our firft connection, that it did not totally agree with your principles and fituation, as you was then married. I admitted every force of this reafoning, knowing how, in one of your exalted character, appearances fhould be fupported: but, my Lord, little did I think when that marriage was diffolved, and the odium which attended our connections confequently fo, that your affections could fo mechanically abate, as in an inftant thus to facrifice

the

Wilkes, if not perfecuted, will foon be forgotten. To be weak and inactive is fafer
than to be daring and criminal; and wide is
the diftance between a riot of the populace
and

the lover to the fordid confiderations of intereft or public opinion.

I CAN readily place your defire of parting with me
to the love of variety; but, my Lord, what am I to fay
to that part of your letter, wherein you infift (as I fhall
forfeit every future claim to your munificence) on my
leaving thefe kingdoms? Am I to attribute it to malevolence or ill-nature? No, my Lord, the actual fuffer-
ing of this fevere fentence (cruel as it is) fhall not wring
from me this confeffion. I will call it the lapfe of the
heart, the fault of conftitution, or any other, fofter
name, that will cover the perfon I hold deareft in the
world, from the unnatural (yet too often affociated)
titles of Seducer and Perfecutor.

MISTAKE me not, my dear Lord, that I want to
plead a remiffion of this fentence from the cruelty
of being driven from my native kingdom (though I
think this fhould have an effect on your feelings) I urge
it on a principle as much more refined as it is diftract-
ing; that of being, for ever, feparated from the Man,
not the Lord, of my choice.

THOUGH my pride won't permit me to fue for the
recovery of a heart, which, I find, is fo obftinately de-
tached from me; yet, my Lord, fuffer me this poor confolation, to live in the fame kingdom with you.—Give
me fome time to mitigate a paffion you firft infpired
me with; and though I find I muft bid adieu to the
transports

and a convulſion of the whole kingdom. You
may live to make the experiment, but no
honeſt man can wiſh you ſhould ſurvive it.

JUNIUS.

LETTER XX.

TO HIS GRACE THE DUKE OF GRAFTON.

MY LORD,.   30 *May* 1769.

I F the meaſures in which you have been
moſt ſuccefsful, had been ſupported by
any tolerable appearance of argument, I
ſhould have thought my time not ill employed, in continuing to examine your conduct as a miniſter, and ſtating it fairly to the
public. But when I ſee queſtions of the

tranſports of love, let me hope for the calmer delights of
friendſhip; and do not, at once, overwhelm me with all
the agonies of poſitive—neglected ſeparation.

You inform me, in the cloſe of your letter, " of
your ſpeedily entering into chaſter connections."—I am
reſigned!—And may your future lady love like me,
but never meet with ſuch returns!—May every hour of
your life be brightened by proſperity; and may the
happineſs of your domeſtic character ever keep pace
with your public one, prays

The unfortunate, &c.

higheſt.

highest national importance, carried as they
have been, and the firft principles of the conftitution. openly violated, without argument
or decency, I confefs, I give up the caufe in
defpair. The meaneft of your predeceffors
had abilities fufficient to give a colour to
their meafures. If they invaded the rights
of the people, they did not dare to offer a
direct infult to their underftanding; and,
in former times, the moft venal parliaments
made it a condition, in their bargain with
the minifter, that he fhould furnifh them
with fome plaufible pretences for felling their
country and themfelves. You have had the
merit of introducing a more compendious
fyftem of government and logic. You neither addrefs yourfelf to the paffions, nor to
the underftanding, but fimply to the touch.
You apply yourfelf immediately to the feelings of your friends, who, contrary to the
forms of parliament, never enter heartily into
a debate, until they have divided.

RELINQUISHING, therefore, all idle views
of amendment to your Grace, or of benefit
to the public, let me be permitted to confider your character and conduct merely as a
fubject of curious fpeculation.——There is
fomething in both, which diftinguifhes you
not only from all other minifters, but all
other men. It is not that you do wrong by
                                    defign,

defign, but that you fhould never do right
by miftake. It is not that your indolence
and your activity have been equally mifap-
plied, but that the firft uniform principle,
or, if I may call it the genius of your life,
fhould have carried you through every poffible change and contradiction of conduct,
without the momentary imputation or colour
of a virtue; and that the wildeft fpirit of inconfiftency fhould never once have betrayed
you into a wife or honourable action. This,
I own, gives an air of fingularity to your
fortune, as well as to your difpofition. Let
us look back together to a fcene, in which
a mind like yours will find nothing to repent
of. Let us try, my Lord, how well you
have fupported the various relations in which
you ftood, to your fovereign, your country,
your friends, and yourfelf. Give us, if it
be poffible, fome excufe to pofterity, and to
ourfelves, for fubmitting to your adminiftration. If not the abilities of a great minifter,
if not the integrity of a patriot, or the fidelity of a friend, fhew us, at leaft the firmnefs of a man.—For the fake of your miftrefs, the lover fhall be fpared. I will not
lead her into public, as you have done, nor
will I infult the memory of departed beauty.
Her fex, which alone made her amiable in
your eyes, makes her refpectable in mine.

THE

The character of the reputed ancestors of some men, has made it possible for their descendants to be vicious in the extreme, without being degenerate. Those of your Grace, for instance, left no distressing examples of virtue, even to their legitimate posterity, and you may look back with pleasure to an illustrious pedigree, in which heraldy has not left a single good quality upon record to insult or upbraid you. You have better proofs of your descent, my Lord, than the register of a marriage, or any troublesome inheritance of reputation. There are some hereditary strokes of character, by which a family may be as clearly distinguished as by the blackest features of the human face. Charles the First lived and died a hypocrite. Charles the Second was a hypocrite of another sort, and should have died upon the same scaffold. At the distance of a century, we see their different characters happily revived, and blended in your Grace. Sullen and severe without religion, profligate without gaiety, you live like Charles the Second, without being an amiable companion, and, for aught I know, may die as his father did, without the reputation of a martyr.

You had already taken your degrees with credit in those schools, in which the English nobility are formed to virtue, when you
were

were introduced to Lord Chatham's protection. From Newmarket, White's, and
the oppofition,* he gave you to the world
with an air of popularity, which young men
ufually fet out with, and feldom prefcrve:
—grave and plaufible enough to be thought
fit for bufinefs; too young for treachery;
and, in fhort, a patriot of no unpromifing expectations. Lord Chatham was the earlieft
object of your political wonder and attachment; yet you deferted him, upon the firft
hopes that offered of an equal fhare of power
with Lord Rockingham. When the Duke
of Cumberland's firft negociation failed, and
when the favourite was pufhed to the laft extremity, you faved him, by joining with an
adminiftration, in which Lord Chatham had
refufed to engage. Still, however, he was
your friend, and you are yet to explain to the

* In March 1763, his Grace was in the Oppofition
to Lord Bute's Adminiftration, and voted againft the
Cyder Bill. In November the fame year he was in the
Oppofition to the Grenville Adminiftration, and protefted
againft the Houfe voting away privilege in cafes of libel.
In 1764 he was a Member of the Minority Club at
Wildman's Tavern in Albemarle Street: this Club, at
its firft inftitution, confifted of 36 Lords and 113 Com-
moners; in all 149; but it foon dwindled away. In
1765 his Grace came in with the Marquis of Rockingham as a fupporter of that nobleman's Adminiftration.
See notes to page 5th.

world,

world, why you confented to act without
him, or why, after uniting with Lord Rockingham, you deferted and betrayed him.
You complained that no meafures were taken
to fatisfy your patron, and that your friend,
Mr. Wilkes, who had fuffered fo much for
the party, had been abandoned to his fate.
They have fince contributed not a little, to
your prefent plenitude of power; yet, I
think, Lord Chatham had lefs reafon than
ever to be fatisfied; and as for Mr. Wilkes,
it is, perhaps, the greateft misfortune of his
life, that you fhould have fo many compenfations to make in the clofet for your former
friendfhip with him. Your gracious mafter
underftands your character, and makes you a
perfecutor, becaufe you have been a friend.

LORD CHATHAM formed his laft adminiftration upon principles which you certainly
concurred in, or you could never have been
placed at the head of the treafury. By deferting thofe principles, and by acting in direct contradiction to them, in which he
found you were fecretly fupported in the
clofet, you foon forced him to leave you to
yourfelf, and to withdraw his name from an
adminiftration, which had been formed on
the credit of it. You had then a profpect
of friendfhips better fuited to your genius,
and more likely to fix your difpofition. Mar-

riage

riage is the point on which every rake is fta-
tionary at laft; and truly, my Lord, you
may well be weary of the circuit you have
taken, for you have now fairly travelled
through every fign in the political zodiac,
from the Scorpion, in which you ftung Lord
Chatham, to the hopes of a Virgin * in the
Houfe of Bloomfbury. One would think
that you had had fufficient experience of the
frailty of nuptial engagements, or, at leaft,
that fuch a friendfhip as the Duke of Bedford's might have been fecured to you by
-the aufpicious marriage of your late Duchefs
with † his nephew. But ties of this tender
nature cannot be drawn too clofe; and it
may poffibly be a part of the Duke of Bedford's ambition, after making her an honeft
woman, to work a miracle of the fame fort
upon your Grace. This worthy Nobleman
has long dealt in virtue. There has been a
large confumption of it in his own family;
and, in the way of traffic, I dare fay, he
has bought and fold more than half the reprefentative integrity of the nation.

* His Grace had lately married Mifs Wrottefley,
niece of the Duchefs of Bedford.

† Miss LIDDELL after being divorced from the
Duke, married the Earl of Upper Offory.

In

' In a political view, this union is not im-
prudent. The favour of princes is a perish-
able commodity. You have now a strength
sufficient to command the closet; and, if it
be necessary to betray one friendship more,
you may set even Lord Bute at defiance. Mr.
Stuart Mackenzie may possibly remember
what use the Duke of Bedford usually makes
of his power; and our gracious Sovereign,
I doubt not, rejoices at this first appearance
of union among his servants. His late Majesty, under the happy influence of a family
connection between his ministers, was relieved from the cares of the government. A
more active prince may perhaps observe,
with suspicion, by what degrees an artful
servant grows upon his master, from the first
unlimited professions of duty and attachment,
to the painful representation of the necessity
of the royal service, and soon, in regular
progression, to the humble insolence of dic-
tating in all the obsequious forms of peremptory submission. The interval is carefully employed in forming connections, cre-
ating interests, collecting a party, and laying
the foundation of double marriages; until the
deluded prince, who thought he had found
a creature prostituted to his service, and in-
significant enough to be always dependent upon his pleasure, finds him at last too strong

to be commanded, and too formidable to be removed.

YOUR Grace's public conduct, as a minister, is but the counter part of your private history;—the same inconsistency, the same contradictions. In America we trace you, from the first opposition to the Stamp Act, on principles of convenience, to Mr. Pitt's surrender of the right; then forward to Lord Rockingham's surrender of the fact; then back again to Lord Rockingham's declaration of the right; then forward to taxation with Mr. Townshend; and in the last instance, from the gentle Conway's undetermined discretion, to blood and compulsion with the Duke of Bedford: Yet if we may believe the simplicity of Lord North's eloquence, at the opening of next sessions you are once more to be the patron of America. Is this the wisdom of a great minister? or is it the ominous vibration of a pendulum? Had you no opinion of your own, my Lord? or was it the gratification of betraying every party with which you have been united, and of deserting every political principle, in which you had concurred?

YOUR enemies may turn their eyes without regret from this admirable system of provincial government. They will find gratification

tion enough in the furvey of your domeſtic
and foreign policy.

IF, inſtead of difowning Lord Shelburne,
the Britiſh court had interpofed with dignity
and firmneſs, you know, my Lord, that Corfica would never have been invaded. The
French ſaw the weaknefs of a diſtracted miniſtry, and were juſtified in treating you
with contempt. They would probably have
yielded in the firſt inſtance, rather than hazard a rupture with this country; but, being
once engaged, they cannot retreat without
diſhonour. Common fenfe forefees confequences, which have eſcaped your Grace's
penetration. Either we ſuffer the French to
make an acquifition, the importance of which
you have probably no conception of, or we
oppofe them by an underhand management,
which only difgraces us in the eyes of Europe, without anſwering any purpofe of policy or prudence. From fecret, indirect
affiſtance, a tranfition to fome more open
decifive meaſures becomes unavoidable; till
at laſt we find ourfelves principal in the war,
and are obliged to hazard every thing for an
object, which might have originally been
obtained without expence or danger. I am
not verfed in the politics of the north; but
this I believe is certain, that half the money
you have diſtributed to carry the expulfion of

F 3   Mr.

Mr. Wilkes, or even your Secretary's fhare in the laft fubfcription, would have kept the Turks at your devotion. Was it œconomy, my Lord? or did the coy refiftance you have conftantly met with in the Britifh fenate, make you defpair of corrupting the Divan? Your friends indeed have the firft claim upon your bounty, but if five hundred pounds a year can be fpared in a penfion to Sir John Moore, it would not have difgraced you to have allowed fomething to the fecret fervice of the public.

You will fay perhaps that the fituation of affairs at home demanded and engroffed the whole of your attention. Here, I confefs, you have been active. An amiable, accomplifhed prince afcends the throne under the happieft of all aufpices, the acclamations and united affections of his fubjects. The firft meafures of his reign, and even the odium of a favourite, were not able to fhake their attachment. Your fervices, my Lord, have been more fuccefsful. Since you were permitted to take the lead, we have feen the natural effects of a fyftem of government, at once both odious and contemptible. We have feen the laws fometimes fcandaloufly relaxed, fometimes violently ftretched beyond their tone. We have feen the perfon of the Sovereign infulted; and in profound peace,

and

and with an undifputed title, the fidelity of his fubjects brought by his own fervants into public queftion. Without abilities, refolution, or intereft, you have done more than Lord Bute could accomplifh with all Scotland at his heels.

Your Grace, little anxious perhaps either for prefent or future reputation, will not defire to be handed down in thefe colours to pofterity. You have reafon to flatter yourfelf that the memory of your adminiftration will furvive even the forms of a conftitution, which our anceftors vainly hoped would be immortal ; and as for your perfonal character, I will not, for the honour of human nature, fuppofe that you can wifh to have it remembered. The condition of the prefent, times is defperate indeed ; but there is a debt due to thofe who come after us, and it is the hiftorian's office to punifh, though he cannot correct. I do not give you to pofterity as a pattern to imitate, but as an example to deter ; and as your conduct comprehends every thing that a wife or honeft minifter fhould avoid, 1 mean to make you a negative inftruction to your fucceffors for ever.

J U N I U S.

LETTER XXI.

TO THE PRINTER OF THE PUBLIC AD-VERTISER.

SIR,　　　　　　　　12 *June*, 1769,

THE Duke of Grafton's friends, not finding it convenient to enter into a conteſt with Junius, are now reduced to the laſt melancholy reſource of defeated argument, the flat general charge of ſcurrility and falſehood. As for his ſtile, I ſhall leave it to the critics. The truth of his faƈts is of more importance to the public. They are of ſuch a nature, that I think a bare contra-diƈtion will have no weight with any man, who judges for himſelf. Let us take them in the order in which they appear in his laſt letter.

1. HAVE not the firſt rights of the people, and the firſt principles of the conſtitution been openly invaded, and the very name of an eleƈtion made ridiculous by the arbitrary appointment of Mr. Luttrell?

2. DID not the Duke of Grafton fre-quently lead his miſtreſs into public, and even

place

place her at the head of his table, as if he had
pulled down an ancient temple of Venus, and
could bury all decency and fhame under the
ruins?—Is this the man who dares to talk of
Mr. Wilkes's morals?

3. Is not the character of his prefumptive
anceftors as ftrongly marked in him, as if he
had defcended from them in a direct legitimate
line? The idea of his death is only 'prophetic; and what is prophecy but a narrative
preceding the fact?

4. WAS not Lord Chatham the firft who
raifed him to the rank and poft of a minifter,
and the firft whom he abandoned?

5. Did he not join with Lord Rockingham, and betray him?

6. WAS he not the bofom friend of Mr.
Wilkes, whom he now purfues to deftruction?

7. DID he not take his degrees with credit
at Newmarket, White's; and the oppofition?

8. AFTER deferting Lord Chatham's principles, and facrificing his friendfhip, is he not
now clofely united with a fet of men, who, tho'
they have occafionally joined with all parties,

have in every different fituation, and at all
times, been equally and conftantly detefted
by this country ?

9. Has not Sir John Moore a penfion of
five hundred pounds a year ?—This may probably be an acquittance of favours upon the
turf.; but is it poffible for a minifter to offer
a groffer outrage to a nation, which has fo
very lately cleared away the beggary of the
civil lift, at the expence of more than half a
million ?

10. Is there any one mode of thinking or
acting with refpect to America, which the
Duke of Grafton has not fucceffively adopted
and abandoned ?

11. Is there not a fingular mark of fhame
fet upon this man, who has fo little delicacy
and feeling as to fubmit to the opprobrium of
marrying a near relation of one who had de-
bauched his wife ?—In the name of decency,
how are thefe amiable coufins to meet at their
uncle's table ?—It will be a fcene in Œdipus,
without the diftrefs.—Is it wealth, or wit, or
beauty,—or is the amorous youth in love ?

THE reft is notorious. That Corfica has
been facrificed to the French: that in fome
inftances the laws have been fcandaloufly relaxed,

laxed, and in others daringly violated ; and that the king's fubjects have been called upon to affure him of their fidelity, in fpite of the meafures of his fervants.

A **WRITER** who builds his arguments upon facts fuch as thefe, is not eafily to be confuted. He is not to be anfwered by general affertions, or general reproaches. He may want eloquence to amufe and perfuade, but, fpeaking truth, he muft always convince.

PHILO JUNIUS.

LETTER XXII.

REPLY TO LETTER XX. SIGNED JUNIUS.

THE author of the letter figned Junius has comprehended all the charges that a difappointed faction, or the malice of his inveterate enemies could invent, againft the private character and family of the Duke of Grafton.

THOSE charges I will anfwer briefly, and for ever after drop the fubject.

1. THE rights of the people were fo far from being invaded in the affair of the elec-

F 6

tion

tion for the county of Middlesex, that not
only two thirds of the nation have in the
most public and solemn manner approved of
that measure, but also the most eminent lawyers in England, with the Chancellor at their
head, declared that the accepting of Mr. Luttrell for member was perfectly legal and constitutional.

2. WHETHER the Duke of Grafton led
his mistress into public is a fact to which I
am an utter stranger; and if he had, there is
scarcely a gentleman in England but has been
at one time or other, seen at a public place
with his female friend.

3. EVERY dispassionate man in the kingdom must own that the weaknesses of the unhappy family, who lost by their folly the
crown of Great Britain, have been too much
exaggerated, and that their crimes proceeded
more from error in judgment, than from any
malignity of mind. They were certainly
more unfortunate than criminal.

4. LORD CHATHAM, it is true, was the
capital figure in the administration in 1766;
but so far was the Duke of Grafton from deserting him, that of his own accord in 1768,
he begged that his name might be taken from
councils, at which the weak state of his
body

body and mind made him incapable to affift.

5. THE Dukc of Grafton during the courfe of Lord Rockingham's adminiftration, faw that the Marquis was altogether unfit for public bufinefs. He did not defert the Marquis, but the Marquis deferted thofe firm principles upon which the Duke wifhed to carry on the bufinefs of the nation.

6. IF the Duke of Grafton was ever acquainted with Mr. Wilkes, it was at a time when the infamy of his character was unknown to the world. To defert the acquaintance of a man deftitute of virtue is real praife: neither can enforcing the law againft the vicious be called perfecution.

7. THE Duke of Grafton was admitted to Newmarket, White's, and oppofition; fo have almoft all the men of family and fafhion in the nation.

8. THAT the Duke of Bedford has ever been detefted by his country, is an abfolute falfehood; fome of his followers have, indeed, been covered with abufe; but their abilities are univerfally allowed, and their honour and patriotifm remain unimpeached.

9. THE

9. THE penfion given to Sir John Moore, does honour to the humanity of the Duke of Grafton, if Sir John has been unfortunate becaufe honeft, it is an act worthy of praife to fupport a numerous family, involved in diftrefs more by the misfortunes, than by the crimes of their parents.

10. ILL underftood, and defignedly involved in obfcurity, the affairs of America bore, at different times, different afpects. The Duke of Grafton has been invariably fixed to ftrike the happy medium between the interefts of America, and the prefervation of the authority of the mother country. If, in the courfe of this defign, he has changed his meafures, we are to attribute this to his prudence, and not to the verfatility of his mind.

THE laft article deferves no anfwer: the factious difpofition of the writer has defeated the defigned effect of his abufe. In one part of his letter he blames his Grace for keeping a miftrefs,—in another for taking a lawful wife. The truth is, faction is determined not to be pleafed. They want to poffefs themfelves of the treafury, and until the Duke refigns that fweet morfel to the devouring jaws of oppofition, it will for ever fpit forth venom and defamation. But the Duke of Grafton defpifes ill founded abufe, as much

much as he abhors the commiffion of the
crime falfely laid to his charge.

OLD NOLL.

LETTER XXIII.

SIR,   22. *June*, 1769.

THE name of Old Noll is deftined to
be the ruin of the houfe of Stuart.
There is an ominous fatality in it, which
even the fpurious defcendants of the family
cannot efcape. Oliver Cromwell had the
merit of conducting Charles the firft to the
block. Your correfpondent Old Noll
appears to have the fame defign upon the
Duke of Grafton. His arguments confift
better with the title he has affumed, than
with the principles he profeffes; for though
he pretends to be an advocate for the Duke,
he takes care to give us the beft reafons, why
his patron fhould regularly follow the fate
of his prefumptive anceftor.—Through the
whole courfe of the Duke of Grafton's life,
I fee a ftrange endeavour to unite contradictions, which cannot be reconciled: He
marries to be divorced:—He keeps a miftrefs

to remind him of conjugal endearments, and
he chooses such friends, as it is virtue in him
to desert.   If it were possible for the genius
of that accomplished president, who pro-
nounced sentence upon Charles the first, to
be revived in some modern sycophant *, his
Grace I doubt not would by sympathy dis-
cover him among the dregs of mankind, and
take him for a guide in those paths, which
naturally conduct a minister to the scaffold.

THE assertion that two-thirds of the nation
approve of the acceptance of Mr. Luttrell (for
even Old Noll is too modest to call it an election) can neither be maintained nor confuted
by argument. It is a point of fact, on which
every English gentleman will determine for
himself.   As to lawyers, their profession is
supported by the indiscriminate defence of
right and wrong, and I confess I have not
that opinion of their knowledge or integrity,
to think it necessary that they should decide
for me upon a plain constitutional question.
With respect to the appointment of Mr. Luttrell, the chancellor has never yet given any
authentic opinion.   Sir Fletcher Norton is
indeed an honest, a very honest man ; and
the Attorney General is *ex officio* the guardian

* Mr. Bradshaw, then secretary to the Treasury.

of liberty, to take care, I prefume, that it
fhall never break out into a criminal excefs.
Doctor Blackftone is Solicitor to the Queen.
The Doctor recollected that he had a place
to preferve, though he forgot that he had a
reputation to lofe. We have now the good
fortune to underftand the Doctor's principles,
as well as writings. For the defence of truth,
of law, and reafon, the Doctor's book may
be fafely confulted ; but whoever wifhes to
cheat a neighbour of his eftate, or to rob a
country of its rights, need make no fcruple
of confulting the Doctor himfelf.

THE example of the Englifh nobility may,
for aught I know, fufficiently juftify the
Duke of Grafton, when he indulges his
genius in all the fafhionable exceffes of the
age ; yet, confidering his rank and ftation, I
think it would do him more honour to be able
to deny the fact, than to defend it by fuch
authority. But if vice itfelf could be excuf-
ed, there is yet a certain difplay of it, a certain outrage to decency, and violation of
public decorum, which, for the benefit of
fociety, fhould never be forgiven. It is not
that he kept a miftrefs at home, but that he
conftantly attended her abroad.—It is not
the private indulgence, but the public infult
of which I complain. The name of Mifs
Parfons would hardly have been known, if
the

the Firſt Lord of the Treaſury had not led
her in triumph through the Opera Houſe,
even in the preſence of the Queen. When
we ſee a man act in this manner, we may admit the ſhameleſs depravity of his heart, but
what are we to think of his underſtanding.

His Grace it ſeems is now to be a regular
domeſtic man, and as an omen of the future
delicacy and correctneſs of his conduct, he
marries a firſt couſin of the man, who had
fixed that mark and title of infamy upon him,
which, at the ſame moment, makes a huſband
unhappy and ridiculous. The ties of con-
ſanguinity may poſſibly preſerve him from
the ſame fate a ſecond time, and as to the
diſtreſs of meeting, I take it for granted the
venerable uncle of theſe common couſins has
ſettled the etiquette in ſuch a manner, that,
if a miſtake ſhould happen, it may reach no
farther than from Madame ma femme to Madame ma couſine.

The Duke of Grafton has always ſome
excellent reaſon for deſerting his friends.—
The age and incapacity of Lord Chatham;
—the debility of Lord Rockingham;—or the
infamy of Mr. Wilkes. There was a time
indeed when he did not appear to be quite ſo
well acquainted, or ſo violently offended with
the infirmities of his friends. But now I confeſs

fefs they are not ill exchanged for the youth-
ful, vigorous virtue of the Duke of Bedford ;—the firmnefs of General Conway ;—
the blunt, or if I may call it, the aukward integrity of Mr. Rigby, and the fpotlefs morality of Lord Sandwich.,

If a late penfion to a * broken gambler be
an act worthy of commendation, the Duke
of Grafton's connexions will furnifh him
with many opportunities of doing praife-worthy actions; and as he himfelf bears no part
of the expence, the generofity of diftributing
the public money for the fupport of virtuous
families in diftrefs will be an unqueftionable
proof of his Grace's humanity.

As to public affairs, Old Noll is a little
tender of defcending to particulars, He does
not deny that ·Corfica has been facrificed to
France, and he confeffes that, with regard
to America, his patron's meafures have been
fubject to fome variation; but then he promifes wonders of ftability and firmnefs for
the future. Thefe are myfteries, of which
we muft not pretend to judge by experience ;
and truly, I fear we fhall perifh in the De-
fart, before we arrive at the Land of Promife.
In the regular courfe of things, the period of

* Sir John Moore.

the

the Duke of Grafton's minifterial manhood
fhould now be approaching. The imbecility
of his infant ftate was committed to Lord
Chatham. Charles Townfhend took fome
care of his education at that ambiguous age,
which lies between the follies of political
childhood, and the vices of puberty. The
empire of the paffions foon fucceeded. His
earlieft principles and connexions were of
courfe forgotten, or defpifed. The company
he has lately kept has been of no fervice to
his morals ; and, in the conduct of public
affairs, we fee the character of his time of
life ftrongly diftinguifhed. An obftinate
ungovernable felf-fufficiency plainly points
out to us that ftate of imperfect maturity, at
which the graceful levity of youth is loft, and
the folidity of experience not yet acquired.
It is poffible the young man may in time grow
wifer and reform ; but, if I underftand his
difpofition, it is not of fuch corrigible ftuff,
that we fhould hope for any amendment in
him; before he has accomplifhed the deftruction of this country. Like other rakes, he
may perhaps live to fee his error, but not un-
till he has ruined his eftate.

PHILO JUNIUS.

LETTER

-

L E T T E R XXIV.

TO HIS GRACE THE DUKE OF GRAFTON.

MY LORD,   8 *July*, 1769.

IF nature had given you an underftanding
qualified to keep pace with the wifhes and
principles of your heart, fhe would have
made you, perhaps, the moft formidable minifter that ever was employed, under a li-
mited monarch, to accomplifh the ruin of a
free people.   When neither the feelings of
fhame, the reproaches of confcience, nor the
dread of punifhment, form any bar to the
defigns of a minifter, the people would have
too much reafon to lament their condition, if
they did not find fome refource in the weaknefs of his underftanding.   We owe it to the
bounty of providence, that the completeft depravity of the heart is fometimes ftrangely
united with a confufion of the mind, which
counteracts the moft favourite principles, and
makes the fame man treacherous without art,
and a hypocrite without deceiving. The meafures, for inftance, in which your Grace's
activity has been chiefly exerted, as they were
adopted without fkill, fhould have been conducted with more than common dexterity.

But

But truly, my Lord, the execution has been as grofs as the defign. By one decifive ftep, you have defeated all the arts of writing. You have fairly confounded the intrigues of oppofition, and filenced the clamours of faction. A dark, ambiguous fyftem might require and furnifh the materials of ingenius illuftration; and, in doubtful meafures, the virulent exaggeration of party muft be employed, to roufe and engage the paffions of the people. You have now brought the merits of your adminiftration to an iffue, on which every Eng--lifhman of the narroweft capacity may determine for himfelf. It is not an alarm to the paffions, but a calm appeal to the judgement of the people, upon their own moft effential interefts. A more experienced minifter, would not have hazarded a direct invafion of the firft principles of the conftitution, before he had made fome progrefs in fubduing the fpirit of the people. With fuch a caufe as yours, my Lord, it is not fufficient that you have the court at your devotion, unlefs you can find means to corrupt or intimidate the jury. The collective body of the people form that jury, and from their decifion there is but one appeal.

WHETHER you have talents to fupport you, at a crifis of fuch difficulty and danger, fhould long fince have been confidered. Judging

ing

ing truly of your difpofition, you have perhaps
miftaken the extent of your capacity. Good
faith and folly have fo long been received as
fynonimous terms, that the reverfe of the propofition has grown into credit, and every villain fancies himfelf a man of abilities. It is
the apprehenfion of your friends, my Lord,
that you have drawn fome hafty conclufion
of this fort, and that a partial reliance upon
your moral character has betrayed you beyond
the depth of your underftanding. You have
now carried things too far to retreat. You
have plainly declared to the people what they
are to expect from the continuance of your
adminiftration. It is time for your Grace to
confider what you alfo may expect in return
from their fpirit and their refentment.

SINCE the acceffion of our moft gracious
Sovereign to the throne, we have feen a fyftem
of government, which may well be called a
reign of experiments. Parties of all denominations have been employed and difmiffed.
The advice of the ableft men in this country
has been repeatedly called for and rejected;
and when the Royal difpleafure has been
fignified to a minifter, the marks of it have
ufually been proportioned to his abilities and
integrity. The fpirit of the Favourite had
fome apparent influence upon every adminiftration; and every fet of minifters preferved

an

an appearance of duration, as long as they
fubmitted to that influence. But there were
certain fervices to be performed for the Favourite's fecurity, or to gratify his refentments, which your predeceffors in office had
the wifdom or the virtue not to undertake.
The moment this refractory fpirit was dif-
covered, their difgrace was determined. Lord
Chatham, Mr. Grenville, and Lord Rockingham have ,fucceffively had the honour to
be difmiffed for preferring their duty, as fervants of the public, to thofe compliances
which were expected from their ftation. A
fubmiffive adminiftration was at laft gradually
collected from the deferters of all parties, interefts, and connexions : and nothing remained but to find a leader for thefe gallant
well-difciplined troops. Stand forth, my
Lord, for thou art the man. Lord Bute found
no refource of dependence or fecurity in the
proud, impofing fuperiority of Lord Chatham's abilities, the fhrewd inflexible judgement of Mr. Grenville, nor in the mild but
determined integrity of Lord Rockingham.
His views and fituation required a creature
void of all thefe properties ; and he was forced
to go through every divifion, refolution, compofition, and refinement of political chemiftry,
before he happily arrived at the caput mor-
tuum of vitriol in your Grace. Flat and infipid in your retired ftate, but brought into

action

action you become vitriol again. Such are
the extremes of alternate indolence or fury,
which have governed your whole adminiftration. Your circumftances with regard
to the people foon becoming defperate, like
other honeft fervants, you determined to involve the beft of mafters in the fame difficulties with yourfelf. We owe it to your
Grace's well-directed labours, that your Sovereign has been perfuaded to doubt of the
affections of his fubjects, and the people to
fufpect the virtues of their Sovereign, at a
time when both were unqueftionable. You
have degraded the Royal dignity into a bafe,
difhonourable competition with Mr. Wilkes,
nor had you abilities to carry even the laft
contemptible triumph over a private man,
without the groffeft violation of the fundamental laws of the conftitution and rights of
the people. But thefe are rights, my Lord,
which you can no more annihilate, than you
can the foil to which they are annexed. The
queftion no longer turns upon points of national honour and fecurity abroad, or on the
degrees of expedience and propriety of meafures at home. It was not inconfiftent that
you fhould abandon the caufe of liberty in
another country, which you had perfecuted
in your own ; and in the common arts of
domeftic corruption, we mifs no part of Sir
Robert Walpole's fyftem, except his abilities.

VOL. I.   G   In

In this humble imitative line, you might long
have proceeded, fafe and contemptible. You
might probably never have rifen to the dignity of being hated, and even have been
defpifed with moderation. But it feems you
meant to be diftinguifhed, and, to a mind like
yours, there was no other road to fame but
by the deftruction of a noble fabric, which
you thought had been too long the admi-
ration of mankind. The ufe you have made
of the military force introduced an alarming
change in the mode of executing the laws.
The arbitrary appointment of Mr. Luttrell
invades the foundation of the laws themfelves,
as it manifeftly transfers the right of legiflation
from thofe whom the people have chofen, to
thofe whom they have rejected. With a fucceffion of fuch appointments, we may foon fee
a houfe of commons collected, in the choice of
which the other towns and counties of England will have as little fhare as the devoted
county of Middlefex.

Yet I truft your Grace will find that
the people of this country are neither to
be intimidated by violent meafures, nor
deceived by refinements. When they fee
Mr. Luttrell feated in the houfe of commons by mere dint of power, and in direct
oppofition to the choice of a whole county,
they will not liften to thofe fubtleties, by
which

which every arbitrary exertion of authority is explained into the law and privilege of parliament. It requires no perfuafion of argument, but fimply the evidence of the fenfes, to convince them, that to transfer the right of election from the collective to the reprefentative body of the people, contradicts all thofe ideas of a houfe of commons, which they have received from their forefathers, and which they had already, though vainly perhaps, delivered to their children. The principles, on which this violent meafure has been defended, have added fcorn to injury, and forced us to feel, that we are not only opprefled but infulted.

WITH what force, my Lord, with what protection, are you prepared to meet the united deteftation of the people of England ? The city of London has given a generous example to the kingdom, in what manner a king of this country ought to be addreffed ; and I fancy, my Lord, it is not yet in your courage to ftand between your Sovereign and the addreffes of his fubjects, The injuries you have done this country are fuch as demand not only redrefs, but vengeance. In vain fhall you look for protection to that venal vote, which you have already paid for —another muft be purchafed ; and to fave a minifter, the houfe of commons muft declare

them-

themfelves not only independent of their con-
ftituents, but the determined enemies of the
conftitution. Confider, my Lord, whether
this be an extremity to which their fears will
permit them to advance; or, if their protection fhould fail you, how far you are authorifed to rely upon the fincerity of thofe
fmiles, which a pious court lavifhes without
reluctance upon a libertine by profeffion. It
is not indeed the leaft of the thoufand contradictions which attend you, that a man,
marked to the world by the groffeft violation
of all ceremony and decorum, fhould be the
firft fervant of a court, in which prayers are
morality, and kneeling is religion. Truft
not too far to appearances, by which your
predeceffors have been deceived, though they
have not been injured. Even the beft of
princes may at laft difcover, that this is a
contention, in which every thing may be
loft, but nothing can be gained; and as you
became minifter by accident, were adopted
without choice, trufted without confidence,
and continued without favour, be affured
that, whenever an occafion preffes, you will
be difcarded without even the forms of regret.
You will then have reafon to be thankful, if
you are permitted to retire to that feat of
learning, which, in contemplation of the
fyftem of your life, the comparative purity of
your manners with thofe of their high ftew-
ard,

ard, and a thoufand other recommending
circumftances, has chofen you to encourage
the growing virtue of their youth, and to
prefide over their education. Whenever the.
fpirit of diftributing prebends and bifhopricks
fhall have departed from you, you will find
that learned feminary perfectly recovered
from the delirium of an inftallation, and,
what in truth it ought to be, once more a
peaceful fcene of flumber and thoughtlefs
meditation. The venerable tutors of the
univerfity will no longer diftrefs your modefty, by propofing you for a pattern to their
pupils. The learned dulnefs of declamation
will be filent ; and even the venal mufe,
though happieft in fiction, will forget your
virtues. Yet, for the benefit of the fucceed-
ing age, I could wifh that your retreat might
be deferred, until your morals fhall happily
be ripened to that maturity of corruption, at
which the worft examples ceafe to he con-
tagious.

LETTER XXV.

TO THE PRINTER OF THE PUBLIC AD-VERTISER.

SIR,   19 *July*, 1769.

A GREAT deal of ufelefs argument might have been faved, in the political conteft, which has arifen from the expulfion of Mr. Wilkes, and the fubfequent appointment of Mr. Luttrell, if the queftion had been once ftated with precifion, to the fatisfaction of each party, and clearly underftood by them both. But in this, as in almoft every other difpute, it ufually happens that much time is loft in referring to a multitude of cafes and precedents, which prove nothing to the purpofe, or in maintaining propofitions, which are either not difputed, or, whether they be admitted or denied, are entirely indifferent as to the matter in debate ; until at laft the mind, perplexed and confounded with the endlefs fubtleties of controverfy, lofes fight of the main queftion, and never arrives at truth. Both parties in the difpute are apt enough to practife thefe difhoneft artifices. The man, who is confcious of the weaknefs of his caufe, is interefted in concealing it : and, on the other

fide,

fide, it is not uncommon to fee a good caufe mangled by advocates, who do not know the real ftrength of it.

. I should be glad to know, for inftance, to what purpo'e, in the prefent cafe, fo many precedents have been produced to prove, that the houfe of commons have a right to expel one of their own members; that it belongs to them to judge of the validity of elections; or that the law of parliament is part of the law of the land? After all thefe propo-fitions are admitted, * Mr. Luttrell's right to his feat will continue to be juft as difputable as it was before. Not one of them is at pre-fent in agitation. Let it be admitted that the houfe of commons were authorifed to ex-pel Mr. Wilkes; that they are the proper court to judge of elections, and that the law of parliament is binding upon the people; ftill it remains to be enquired whether the houfe, by their refolution in favour of Mr. Luttrell, have or have not truly declared that law. To facilitate this enquiry, I would have the queftion cleared of all foreign or in-different matter. The following ftate of it will probably be thought a fair one by both parties; and then I imagine there is no

* They are only admitted, for the fake of argument, and to bring the queftion to iffue.

gentle-

gentleman in this country, who will not be capable of forming a judicious and true opinion upon it. I take the question to be strictly this : " Whether or no it be the " known, established law of parliament, that " the expulsion of a member of the house " of commons of itself creates in him such " an incapacity to be re-elected, that, at a " subsequent election, any votes given to " him are null and void, and that any other " candidate, who, except the person expel- " led, has the greatest number of votes, ought " to be the sitting member."

To prove that the affirmative is the law of parliament, I apprehend it is not sufficient for the present house of commons to declare it to be so. We may shut our eyes indeed to the dangerous consequences of suffering one branch of the legislature to declare new laws, without argument or example, and it may perhaps be prudent enough to submit to authority ; but a mere assertion will never convince, much less it will be thought reasonable to prove the right by the fact itself. The ministry have not yet pretended to such a tyranny over our minds. To support the affirmative fairly, it will either be necessary to produce some statute, in which that positive provision shall have been made, that specific disability clearly created, and the con-

sequences

fequences of it declared ; or, if there be no
fuch ftatute, the cuftom of parliament muft
then be referred to, and fome cafe or cafes *,
ftrictly in point, muft be produced, with
the decifion of the court upon them: for I
readily admit that the cuftom of parliament,
once clearly proved, is equally binding with
the common and ftatute law.

THE confideration of what may be reafonable or unreafonable makes no part of this
queftion. We are enquiring what the law
is, not what it ought to be. Reafon may
be applied to fhew the impropriety or expedience of a law, but we muft have either
ftatute or precedent to prove the exiftence of
it. At the fame time I do not mean to admit
that the late refolution of the houfe of commons is defenfible on general principles of
reafon, any more than in law. This is not
the hinge on which the debate turns.

SUPPOSING therefore that I have laid down
an accurate ftate of the queftion, I will venture to affirm, 1ft, That there is no ftatute
exifting by which that fpecific difability
which we fpeak of is created. If there be,

* Junius thought it neceffary to meet miniftry on
their own ground ; though precedents in oppofition to
principles, have little weight with him.

G 5   let

let it be produced. The argument will then be at an end.

2dly, THAT there is no precedent in all the proceedings of the houfe of commons which comes entirely home to the prefent cafe, viz. " where an expelled member has " been returned again, and another candi- " date, with an inferior number of votes, " has been declared the fitting member." If there be fuch a precedent, let it be given to us plainly, and I am fure it will have more weight than all the cunning arguments which have been drawn from inferences and probabilities.

THE miniftry, in that laborious pamphlet which I prefume contains the whole ftrength of the party, have declared*, " That Mr. " Walpole's was the firft and only inftance, " in which the electors of any county or bo- " rough had returned a perfon expelled to " ferve in the fame parliament." It is not poffible to conceive a cafe more exactly in point. Mr. Walpole was expelled, and, having a majority of votes at the next election, was returned again. The friends of Mr. Taylor, a candidate fet up by the miniftry, petitioned the houfe that he might

* Cafe of the Middlefex election confidered, page 38.

be

be the fitting member. Thus far the circumftances tally exactly, except that our
houfe of commons faved Mr. Luttrell the
trouble of petitioning. The point of law
however was the fame. It came regularly
before the houfe, and it was their bufinefs
to determine upon it. They did determine
it, for they declared Mr. Taylor *not duly
elected.* If it be faid that they meant this
refolution as matter of favour and indulgence to the borough, which had retorted
Mr. Walpole upon them, in order that the
burgefles, knowing what the law was, might
correct their error. I anfwer,

I. THAT it is a ftrange way of arguing to
oppofe a fuppofition, which no man can
prove, to a fact which proves itfelf.

II. THAT if this were the intention of the
houfe of commons, it muft have defeated itfelf. The burgefles of Lynn could never
have known their error, much lefs could they
have corrected it by any inftruction they received from the proceedings of the houfe of
commons. They might perhaps have forefeen, that, if they returned Mr. Walpole
again, he would again be rejected; but they
never could infer, from a refolution by which
the candidate with the feweft votes was declared *not duly elected,* that, at a future elec-

G 6   tion

tion, and in fimilar circumftances, the houfe
of commons would reverfe their refolution,
and receive the fame candidate as duly elected, whom they had before rejected.

THIS indeed would have been a moft extraordinary way of declaring the law of parliament, and what I prefume no man, whofe
underftanding is not at crofs purpofes with
itfelf, could poffibly underftand.

IF, in a cafe of this importance, I thought
myfelf at liberty to argue from fuppofitions
rather than from facts, I think the probability, in this inftance, is directly the reverfe
of what the miniftry affirm; and that it is
much more likely that the houfe of commons
at that time would rather have ftrained a
point in favour of Mr. Taylor, than that
they would have violated the law of parliament, and robbed Mr. Taylor of a right
legally vefted in him, to gratify a refractory
borough, which in defiance of them, had
returned a perfon branded with the ftrongeft
mark of the difpleafure of the houfe.

BUT really, Sir, this way of talking, for
I cannot call it argument, is a mockery of
the common underftanding of the nation, too
grofs to be endured. Our deareft interefts
are at ftake. An attempt has been made, not
merely

merely to rob a fingle county of its rights, but, by inevitable confequence, to alter the conftitution of the houfe of commons. . This fatal attempt has fucceeded, and ftands as a precedent recorded for ever. If the miniftry are unable to defend their caufe by fair ar-. gument founded on facts, let them fpare us at leaft the mortification of being amufed and deluded like children. I believe there is yet - a fpirit of refiftance in this country, which will not fubmit to be oppreffed; but I am. fure there is a fund of good fenfe in this country, which cannot be deceived.

J U N I U S.

L E T T E R XXVI.

T.O T H E P R I N T E R O F T H E P U B L I C
A D V E R T I S E R..

S I. R,,   1 *Auguft*, 1769.

IT will not be neceffary for *Junius* to take the trouble of anfwering your correfpondent G. A. or the quotation from a fpeech without doors, publifhed in your paper of the 28th of laft month. The fpeech appeared before *Junius*'s letter, and as the author feems to confider the great propofition,, on which all his argument depends, viz. *that Mr. Wilkes*

was

was under that known legal incapacity, of which Junius speaks, as a point granted, his speech is, in no shape, an answer to *Junius,* for this is the very question in debate.

As to G. A. I observe first, that if he did not admit *Junius's* state of the question, he should have shewn the fallacy of it, or given us a more exact one;—secondly, that, considering the many hours and days, which the ministry and their advocates have wasted, in public debate, in compiling large quartos, and collecting innumerable precedents, expressly to prove that the late proceedings of the house of commons are warranted by the law, custom, and practice of parliament, it is rather an extraordinary supposition, to be made by one of their own party even for the sake of argument, *that no such statute, no such custom of parliament, no such case in point can be produced.* G. A. may however make the supposition with safety. It contains nothing, but literally the fact, except that there is a case exactly in point, with a decision of the house diametrically opposite to that which the present house of commons came to in favour of Mr. Luttrell.

The ministry now begin to be ashamed of the weakness of their cause, and, as it usually happens with falsehood, are driven to the necessity

ceffity of fhifting their ground, and changing
their whole defence. At firft we were told
that nothing could be clearer than that the
proceedings of the houfe of commons were
juftified by the known law and uniform cuftom of parliament. But now it feems, if
there be no law, the houfe of commons have
a right to make one, and if there be no precedent, they have a right to create the firft ;
—for this I prefume is the amount of the
queftions propofed to *Junius*. If your correfpondent had been at all verfed in the law
of parliament, or generally in the laws of this
country, he would have feen that this defence
is as weak and falfe as the former.

THE privileges of either houfe of parliament, it is true, are indefinite, that is, they
have not been defcribed or laid down in any
one code or declaration whatfoever; but
whenever a queftion of privilege has arifen,
it has invariably been difputed or maintained
upon the footing of precedents alone*. In
the courfe of the proceedings upon the Aylef-
bury election, the houfe of lords' refolved,
" That neither houfe of parliament had any
" power, by any vote or declaration, to

---

* This is again meeting miniftry upon their own
ground; but precedents cannot vindicate either natural
injuftice, or violation of pofitive right.

" create,

" create to themselves any new privilege that
" was not warranted by the known laws and
" cuftoms of parliament." And to this rule
the houfe of commons, though otherwife
they had acted in a very arbitrary manner,
gave their affent, for they affirmed that they
had guided themfelves by it, in afferting their
privileges.—Now, Sir, if this be true with
refpect to matters of privilege, in which the
houfe of commons, individually and as a
body, are principally concerned, how much
more ftrongly will it hold againft any pretended power in that houfe, to create or declare a new law, by which not only the
rights of the houfe over their own member,
and thofe of the member himfelf are included, but alfo thofe of a third and feparate
party, I mean the freeholders of the kingdom. To do juftice to the miniftry, they
have not yet pretended that any one or any
two of the three eftates have power to make
a new law, without the concurrence of the
third. They know that a man who main-
tains fuch a doctrine is liable, by ftatute, to
the heavieft penalties. They do not acknowledge that the houfe of commons have
affumed a *new* privilege, or declared a *new*
law. On the contrary, they affirm that their
proceedings have been ftrictly conformable to,
and founded upon, the ancient law and cuftom of parliament. Thus therefore the
                                    queftion

queftion returns to the point, at which *Ju-nius* had fixed it, viz. *Whether or no this be the law of parliament.* If it be not, the houfe of commons had no legal authority to eftablifh the precedent; and the precedent itfelf is a mere fact, without any proof of right whatfoever.

Your correfpondent concludes with a queftion of the fimpleft nature: *Muft a thing be wrong, becaufe it has never been done before?* No. But admitting it were proper to be done, that alone does not convey an authority to do it. As to the prefent cafe, I hope I fhall never fee the time, when not only a fingle perfon, but a whole county, and in effect the entire collective body of the people, may again be robbed of their birthright by a vote of the houfe of commons. But if, for reafons which I am unable to comprehend, it be neceffary to truft that houfe with a power fo exorbitant and fo unconftitutional, at leaft let it be given to them by an act of the legiflature.

PHILO JUNIUS.

LETTER

LETTER XXVII.

TO SIR WILLIAM BLACKSTONE SOLICITOR GENERAL TO HER MAJESTY.

·S I R, 29 *July*, 1769.

I SHALL make you no apology for confidering a certain pamphlet*, in which your late conduct is defended, as written by yourfelf, the perfonal interefts, the perfonal refentments, and above all, that wounded fpirit, unaccuftomed to reproach, and I hope not frequently confcious of deferving it, are fignals which betray the author to us as plainly as if your name were in the title-page. You appeal to the public in defence of your reputation. We hold it, Sir, that an injury offered to an individual is interefting to fociety. On this principle the people of England made common caufe with Mr. Wilkes. On this principle, if *you* are injured, they will join in your refentment. I fhall not follow you through the infipid form of a third perfon, but addrefs myfelf to you directly.

* A LETTER to the Author of the Queftion Stated.

You

You feem to think the channel of a pamphlet more refpectable and better fuited to the
dignity of your caufe, than that of a newf-
paper. Be it fo. Yet if newfpapers are
fcurrilous, you muft confefs they are impartial. They give us, without any apparent
preference, the wit and argument of the miniftry, as well as the abufive dulnefs of the
oppofition. The fcales are equally poifed.
It it not the printer's fault if the greater
weight inclines the balance.

. Your pamphlet then is divided into an
attack upon Mr. Grenville's character, and
a defence of your own. It would have been
more confiftent perhaps with your profeffed
intention, to have confined yourfelf to the
laft. But anger has fome claim to indulgence, and railing is ufually a relief to
the mind. I hope you have found benefit
from the experiment. It is not my defign to enter into a formal vindication of
Mr. Grenville, upon his own principles.
I have neither the honour of being perfonally known to him, nor do I pretend to be
completely mafter of all the facts. I need
not run the rifque of doing an injuftice to
his opinions, or to his conduct, when your
pamphlet alone carries, upon the face of it,
a full vindication of both.

YOUR

YOUR firſt reflection is, that Mr. Grenville * was, of all men, the perſon, who
ſhould not have complained of inconſiſtence
with regard to Mr. Wilkes. This, Sir, is
either an unmeaning ſneer, a peeviſh expreſſion of reſentment, or, if it means any
thing, you plainly beg the queſtion ; for whether his parliamentary conduct with regard
to Mr. Wilkes has or has not been incon-
ſiſtent, remains yet to be proved. But it
ſeems he received upon the ſpot a ſufficient
chaſtiſement for exerciſing *ſo unfairly* his talents of miſrepreſentation. You are a lawyer,
Sir, and know better than I do, upon what
particular occaſions a talent for miſrepreſentation may be *fairly* exerted; but to pu-
niſh a man a ſecond time, when he has been
once ſufficiently chaſtiſed, is rather too ſevere. It is not in the laws of England; it
is not in your own commentaries, nor is it
yet, I believe, in the new law you have re-
vealed to the houſe of commons. I hope this
doctrine has no exiſtence but in your own
heart. After all, Sir, if you had conſulted
that ſober diſcretion, which you ſeem to op-
poſe with triumph to the honeſt jollity of a

---

* DR. BLACKSTONE while ſpeaking in the houſe
had not his own excellent Commentaries in view; and
Mr. Grenville, who replied to him, quoted a paſſage
from them, which directly contradicted the doctrine
maintained by the Doctor in his ſpeech.

tavern

tavern, it might have occurred to you that, although you could have fucceeded in fixing a charge of inconfiftence upon Mr. Grenville, it would not have tended in any fhape to exculpate yourfelf.

Your next infinuation, that Sir William Meredith had haftily adopted the falfe glofles of his new ally, is of the fame fort with the firft. It conveys a fneer as little worthy of the gravity of your character, as it is ufelefs to your defence. It is of little moment to the public to enquire, by whom the charge was conceived, or by whom it was adopted. The only queftion we afk is, whether or no it be true. The remainder of your reflections upon Mr. Grenville's conduct deftroy themfelves. He could not poffibly come prepared to traduce your integrity to the houfe. He could not forefee that you would even fpeak upon the queftion, much lefs could he forefee that you would maintain a direct contradiction of that doctrine, which you had folemnly, difinterestedly, and upon fobereft reflection delivered to the public. He came armed indeed with what he thought a refpectable authority, to fupport what he was convinced was the caufe of truth, and I doubt not, he intended to give you, in the courfe of the debate, an honourable and public teftimony of his efteem. Thinking high-

ly

ly of his abilities, I cannot however allow him the gift of divination. As to what you are pleafed to call a plan coolly formed to impofe upon the houfe of commons, and his producing it without provocation at midnight, I confider it as the language of pique and invective, therefore unworthy of regard. But, Sir, I am fenfible I have followed your example too long, and wandered from the point.

THE quotation from your commentaries is matter of record. It can neither be *altered* by your friends, nor mifreprefented by your enemies; and I am willing to take your own word for what you have faid in the houfe of commons. If there be a real difference between what you have written and what you have fpoken, you confefs that your book ought to be the ftandard. Now, Sir, if words mean any thing, I apprehend that, when a long enumeration of difqualifications (whether by ftatute or the cuftom of parliament) concludes with thefe general comprehenfive words, " but fubject to thefe reftric-
" tions and difqualifications, *every* fubject of
" the realm is eligible of common right," a reader of plain underftanding muft of courfe reft fatisfied, that no fpecies of difqualification whatfoever had been omitted. The known character of the author, and the apparent

parent accuracy with which the whole work
is compiled, would confirm him in his opinion; nor could he poſſibly form any other
judgment, without looking upon your commentaries in the ſame light in which you
conſider thoſe penal laws, which though not
repealed, are fallen into diſuſe, and are now
in effect A SNARE TO THE UNWARY*.

You tell us indeed that it was not part of
your plan to ſpecify any temporary incapacity, and that you could not, without a ſpirit
of prophecy, have ſpecified the diſability of a
private individual, ſubſequent to the period
at which you wrote. What your plan was
I know not; but what it ſhould have been,
in order to complete the work you have given
us, is by no means difficult to determine.
The incapacity, which you call temporary,
may continue ſeven years; and though you
might not have foreſeen the particular caſe
of Mr. Wilkes, you might and ſhould have
foreſeen the poſſibility of *ſuch* a caſe, and told
us how far the houſe of commons were au-
thoriſed to proceed in it by the law and cuſtom of parliament. The freeholders of Mid-

* IF a Judge in ſtating the law upon any point, affirms that he has included every caſe, and it appears
afterwards that he had purpoſely omitted a material
caſe, he, in effect, lays *a ſnare for the unwary.*

dleſex

dlefex would then have known what they had
to truft to, and would never have returned
Mr. Wilkes, when Colonel Luttrell was a
candidate againft him. They would have
chofen fome indifferent perfon, rather than
fubmit to be reprefented by the object of their
contempt and deteftation.

YOUR attempt to diftinguifh between difa-
bilities, which affect whofe claffes of men, and
thofe which affect individuals only, is really
unworthy of your underftanding. Your commentaries had taught me that, although the
inftance, in which a penal law is exerted,
be particular, the laws themfelves are general. They are made for the benefit and inftruction of the public, though the penalty
falls only upon an individual. You cannot
but know, Sir, that what was Mr. Wilkes's
cafe yefterday may be your's or mine to-
morrow, and that confequently, the common right of every fubject of the realm is invaded by it. Profeffing therefore to treat of
the conftitution of the houfe of commons,
and of the laws and cuftoms relative to that
conftitution, you certainly were guilty of a
moft unpardonable omiffion in taking no notice of a right and privilege of the houfe,
more extraordinary and more arbitrary than
all the others they poffefs put together. If
the expulfion of a member, not under any

legal

legal difability, of itfelf creates in him an
incapacity to be elected, I fee a ready way
marked out, by which the majority may at·
any time remove the honefteft and ableft men
who happen to be in oppofition to them.
To fay that they *will not* make this extravagant ufe of their power, would be a language unfit for a man fo learned in the laws
as you are. ·By your doctrine, Sir, they *have*
the power, and laws you know are intended
to guard againft what men *may* do, not to
truft to what they *will* do.

Upon the whole, Sir, the charge againft
you is of a plain, fimple nature : It appears
even upon the face of your own pamphlet. On the contrary, your juftification of
yourfelf is full of fubtlety and refinement,
and in fome places not very intelligible. ·
If I were perfonally your enemy, I fhould
dwell, with a malignant pleafure, upon thofe
great and ufeful qualifications, which you
certainly poflefs, and by which you once acquired though they could not preferve to you
the refpect and efteem of your country. I
fhould enumerate the honours you have loft,
and the virtues you have difgraced : but
having no private refentments to gratify, I
think it fufficient to have given my opinion
of your public conduct, leaving the pu-

nifhment it deferves to your clofet and to yourfelf.

JUNIUS.

LETTER XXVIII.

TO THE PRINTER OF THE PUBLIC ADVERTISER.

SIR, 14 *Auguſt*, 1769.

A CORRESPONDENT of the St. James's Evening Poſt firſt wilfully mifunderſtands Junius, then cenfures him for a bad reafoner. Junius does not fay that it was incumbent upon Doctor Blackſtone to forefee and ſtate the crimes, for which Mr. Wilkes was expelled. If, by a fpirit of prophecy, he had even done fo, it would have been nothing to the purpofe. The queſtion is, not for what particular offences a perfon may be expelled, but generally whether by the law of parliament expulfion alone creates a difqualification. If the affirmative be the law of parliament, Doctor Blackſtone might and fhould have told us fo. The queſtion is not confined to this or that particular perfon, but forms one great general branch of difqualification, too important in itfelf, and too extenfive in its confequences, to be omitted in an accurate work exprefsly treating of the law of parliament.

THE

THE truth of the matter is evidently this, Doctor Blackstone, while he was speaking in the house of commons, never once thought of his Commentaries, until the contradiction was unexpectedly urged, and stared him in the face. Instead of defending himself upon the spot, he sunk under the charge, in an agony of confusion and despair. It is well known that there was a pause of some minutes in the house, from a general expectation that the Doctor would say something in his own defence ; but it seems, his faculties were too much overpowered to think of those subtleties and refinements, which have since occurred to him. It was then Mr. Grenville received that severe chastisement, which the Doctor mentions with so much triumph. *I wish the honourable gentleman, instead of shaking his head, would shake a good argument out of it.* If to the elegance, novelty, and bitterness of this ingenious sarcasm, we add the natural melody of the amiable Sir Fletcher Norton's pipe, we shall not be surprised that Mr. Grenville was unable to make him any reply.

As to the Doctor, I would recommend it to him to be quiet. If not, he may perhaps hear again from Junius himself.

PHILO JUNIUS.

POSTSCRIPT XXIX.

TO A PAMPHLET INTITLED, ' AN AN-
' SWER TO THE QUESTION STATED.'
SUPPOSED TO BE WRITTEN BY DR.
BLACKSTONE, SOLICITOR TO THE
QUEEN, IN ANSWER TO JUNIUS'S
LETTER. NO. XXV.

SINCE thefe papers were fent to the prefs, a writer in the public papers, who fub-fcribes himfelf Junius, has made a feint of bringing this queftion to a fhort iffue. Though the foregoing obfervations contain in my opinion, at leaft, a full refutation of all that this writer has offered, I fhall, however, beftow a very few words upon him. It will coft me very little trouble to unravel and expofe the fophiftry of his argument.

' I TAKE the queftion, fays he, to be ftrictly
' this : Whether or no it be the known efta-
' blifhed law of parliament, that the expulfion
' of a member of the houfe of commons of
' itfelf creates in him fuch an incapacity to be
' re-elected, that, at a fubfequent election,
' any votes given to him are null and void ;
' and that any other candidate, who, except
the

' the perfon expelled, has the greateft number
' of votes, ought to be the fitting member.'

WAVING for the prefent any objection I
may have to this ftate of the queftion, I fhall
venture to meet our champion upon his own
ground ; and attempt to fupport the affirmative of it, in one of the two ways, by which
he fays it can be alone fairly fupported. ' If
' there be no ftatute, fays he, in which the
' fpecific difability is clearly created, &c. (and
' we acknowledge there is none) the cuftom
' of parliament muft then be referred to, and
' fome cafe or cafes, ftrictly in point, muft
' be produced, with the decifion of the court
' upon them.' Now I affert, that this has
been done. Mr. Walpole's cafe is ftrictly
in point, to prove that expulfion creates abfolute incapacity of being re-elected. This
was the clear decifion of the houfe upon it.;
and was a full declaration, that incapacity was
the neceffary confequence of expulfion. The
law was as clearly and firmly fixed by this
refolution, and is as binding in every fubfequent cafe of expulfion, as if it had been declared by an exprefs ftatute, " That a mem-
" ber expelled by a refolution of the houfe
" of commons fhall be deemed incapable of
" being re-elected." Whatever doubt then
there might have been of the law before Mr.
Walpole's cafe, with refpect to the full ope-

ration

ration of a vote of expulfion, there can be
none now. The decifion of the houfe upon
this cafe is ftri&ly in point to prove, that
expulfion creates abfolute incapacity in law of
being re-elected.

BUT incapacity in law in this inftance
muft have the fame operation and effect with
incapacity in law in every other inftance.
Now, incapacity of being re-elected implies
in its very terms, that any votes given to the
incapable perfon at a fubfequent election are
null and void. This is its neceffary operation, or it has no operation at all. It is
vox et præterea nihil. We can no more be
called upon to prove this propofition, than
we can to prove that a dead man is not
alive, or that twice two are four. When
the terms are underftood, the propofition is
felf-evident.

LASTLY, It is in all cafes of election the
known and eftablifhed law of the land,
grounded upon the cleareft principles of reafon and common fenfe, that if the votes given
to one candidate are null and void, they cannot be oppofed to the votes given to another
candidate. They cannot affect the votes of
fuch candidate at all. As they have, on the
one hand, no pofitive quality to add or eftablifh, fo have they, on the other hand, no negative

gative one to fubftract or deftroy. They are,
in a word, a mere non-entity. Such was the
determination of the houfe of commons in the
Malden and Bedford elections; cafes ftrictly
in point to the prefent queftion, as far as they
are meant to be in point. And to fay, that
they are not in point, in all circumftances, in
thofe particularly which are independent of
the propofition which they are quoted to '
prove, is to fay no more than that Malden
is not Middlefex, nor Serjeant Comyns Mr.
Wilkes.

LET us fee then how our proof ftands. Expulfion creates incapacity ; incapacity anni-
hilates any votes given to the incapable perfon. The votes given to the qualified candidate ftand upon their own bottom, firm,
and untouched, and can alone have effect.
This, one would think, would be fufficient.
But we are ftopped fhort, and told, that none
of our precedents come home to the prefent
cafe ; and are challenged to produce " a pre-
" cedent in all the proceedings of the houfe
" of commons that does come home to it,
" viz. *where an expelled member has been re-*
" *turned again, and another candidate, with an*
" *inferior number of votes, has been declared*
" *the fitting member.*"

H 4.   INSTEAD

INSTEAD of a precedent, I will beg leave
to put a cafe; which, I fancy, will be quite
as decifive to the prefent point. Suppofe
another Sacheverel, (and every party mult
have its Sacheverel) fhould, at fome future
election, take it in his head to offer himfelf a candidate for the county of Middlefex.
He is oppofed by a candidate, whofe coat is
of a different colour; but however of a very
good colour. The divine has an indifpu-
table majority: nay, the poor layman is abfolutely diftanced. The fheriff, after having
had his confcience well informed by the re-
verend cafuift, returns him, as he fuppofes,
duly elected. The whole houfe is in an up-
roar, at the apprehenfion of fo ftrange an appearance amongft them. A motion however
is at length made, that the perfon was incapable of being elected, that his election therefore is null and void, and that his competitor
ought to have been returned. No, fays a
great orator, firft, fhew me your law for
this proceeding. " Either produce me a fta-
" tute, in which the fpecific difability of a
" clergyman is created; or, produce me a
" precedent *where a clergyman has been re-*
" *turned, and another candidate, with an inferior*
" *number of votes, has been declared the fitting*
" *member.*" No fuch ftatute, no fuch precedent to be found. What anfwer then is
to be given to this demand? The very fame
anfwer

anfwer which I will give to that of Junius:
That there is more than one precedent in the
proceedings of the houfe——" where an in-
" capable perfon has been returned, and an-
" other candidate, with an inferior number of
" votes, has been declared the fitting mem-
" ber; and that this is the known and efta-
" blifhed law, in all cafes of incapacity, from
" whatever caufe it may arife."

· I SHALL now therefore beg leave to make
a flight amendment to Junius's ftate of the
queftion, the affirmative of which will then
ftand thus:

" IT is the known and eftablifhed law of
" parliament, that the expulfion of any mem-
" ber of the houfe of commons creates in
" him an incapacity of being re-elected;
" that any votes given to him at a fubfe-
" quent election are, in confequence of fuch
" incapacity, null and void; and that any
" other candidate, who, except the perfon
" rendered incapable, has the greateft number
" of votes, ought to be the fitting member."

BUT our bufinefs is not yet quite finifhed.
Mr. Walpole's cafe muft have a re-hearing.
" It is not poffible, fays this writer, to con-
" ceive a cafe more exactly in point. Mr.
" Walpole was expelled, and having a majo-

" rity

" rity of votes at the next election, was re-
" turned again. The friends of Mr. Taylor,
" a candidate set up by the ministry, peti-
" tioned the house that he might be the sitting
" member. Thus far the circumstances
" tally exactly, except that our house of
" commons saved Mr. Luttrell the trouble
" of petitioning. The point of law, how-
" ever, was the same. It came regularly be-
" fore the house, and it was their business to
" determine upon it. They did determine
" it; for they declared Mr. Taylor *not duly*
" *elected.*"

. Instead of examining the justness of this
representation, I shall beg leave to oppose
against it my own view of this case, in as
plain a manner and as few words as I am
able.

It was the known and established law of
parliament, when the charge against Mr.
Walpole came before the house of commons,
that they had power to expel, to disable, and
to render incapable for offences. In virtue of
this power they expelled him.

Had they, in the very vote of expulsion,
adjudged him, in terms, to be incapable of
being re-elected, there must have been at
once an end with him. But though the right
of

of the houfe, both to expel, and adjudge incapable, was clear and indubitable, it does
not appear to me, that the full operation. and
effect of a vote of expulfion fingly was fo..
The law in this cafe had never been exprefsly declared. There had been no event
to call up fuch a declaration. I trouble not
myfelf with the grammatical meaning of the
word expulfion. I regard only its legal
meaning. This was not, as I think, pre-
cifely fixed. The houfe thought proper
to fix it; and explicitly to declare the full
confequences of their former vote, before they
fuffered thefe confequences to take effect.
And in this proceeding they acted upon the
moft liberal and folid principles of equity,
juftice and law. What then did the burgeffes of Lynn collect from this fecond vote?
Their fubfequent conduct will tell us: it will
with certainty tell us, that they confidered it
as decifive againft Mr. Walpole; it will alfo,
with equal certainty, tell us, that, upon fuppofition that the law of election ftood then,
as it does now, and that they knew it to ftand
thus, they inferred, " that at a future elec-
" tion, and in cafe of a fimilar return, the
" houfe would receive the fame candidate, as
" duly elected, whom they had before reject-
" ed." They could infer nothing but this.

H.6

It

It is needlefs to repeat the circumftance
of diffimilarity in the prefent cafe. It will
be fufficient to obferve, that as the law of
parliament, upon which the houfe of commons grounded every ftep of their proceedings, was clear beyond the reach of doubt,
fo neither could the freeholders of Middlefex be at a lofs to forefee what muft be the
Inevitable confequence of their proceedings
'in oppofition to it. For upon every return
of Mr. Wilkes, the houfe made enquiry,
whether any votes were given to any other
candidate ?

But I could venture, for the experiment's
fake, even to give this writer the utmoft he
afks ; to allow the moft perfect fimilarity
throughout in thefe two cafes ; to allow,
that the law of expulfion was quite as clear
to the burgeffes of Lynn, as to the freeholders of Middlefex. It will, I am confi-
dent, avail his caufe but little. It will only
prove, that, the law of election at that time
was different from the prefent law. It
will prove, that, in all cafes of an incapable
candidate returned, the law then was, that
the whole election fhould be void. But now
we know that this is not law. The cafes of
Malden and Bedford were, as has been feen,
determined upon other and more juft principles,

ples. And thefe determinations are, I imagine, admitted on all fides, to be law.

I WOULD willingly draw a veil over the
remaining part of this paper. It is aftonifh-
ing, it is painful, to fee men of parts and ability, giving into the moft unworthy artifices,
and defcending fo much below their true line
of character. But if they are not the dupes
of their fophiftry, (which is hardly to be conceived) let them confider that they are fomething much worfe.

THE deareft interefts of this country are
its laws and its conftitution. Againft every
attack upon thefe, there will, I hope, be always found amongft us the firmeft *fpirit of
refiftance*; fuperior to the united efforts of
faction and ambition. For ambition, though
it does not always take the lead of faction,
will be fure in the end to make the moft fatal advantage of it, and draw it to its own
purpofes. But, I truft, our day of trial is
yet far off; and there is *a fund of good fenfe in
this country, which cannot long be deceived,* by
the arts either of falfe reafoning or falfe patriotifm.

LETTER XXX.

TO THE PRINTER OF THE PUBLIC AD-
VERTISER.

S I R,   8 *Auguſt*, 1769.

THE gentleman, who has publiſhed an
answer * to Sir William Meredith's
pamphlet, having honoured me with a poſt-
ſcript of ſix quarto pages, which he mo-
derately calls, beſtowing a *very* few words
upon me, I cannot, in common politeneſs,
refuſe him a reply. The form and magnitude
of a quarto impoſes upon the mind ; and men,
who are unequal to the labour of diſcuſſing
an intricate argument, or wiſh to avoid it,
are willing enough to ſuppoſe, that much has
been proved, becauſe much has been ſaid.
Mine, I confeſs, are humble labours. I do
not preſume to inſtruct the learned, but ſim-
ply to inform the body of the people; and I
prefer that channel of conveyance, which is
likely to ſpread fartheſt among them. The
advocates of the miniſtry ſeem to me to write
for fame, and to flatter themſelves, that the

---

* This pamphlet is entitled, " *An Anſwer to the
Queſtion Stated.*"

ſize

size of their works will make them immortal. They pile up reluctant quarto upon solid folio, as if their labours, because they are gigantic, could contend with truth and heaven.

The writer of the volume in question meets me upon my own ground. He acknowledges there is no statute, by which the specific disability we speak of is created, but he affirms, that the custom of parliament has been referred to, and that a case strictly in point has been produced, with the decision of the court upon it.—I thank him for coming so fairly to the point. He asserts, that the case of Mr. Walpole is strictly in point to prove that expulsion creates an absolute incapacity of being re-elected; and for this purpose he refers generally to the first vote of the house upon that occasion, without venturing to recite the vote itself. The unfair, disingenuous artifice of adopting that part of a precedent, which seems to suit his purpose, and omitting the remainder, deserves some pity, but cannot excite my resentment. He takes advantage eagerly of the first resolution, by which Mr. Walpole's incapacity is declared; but as to the two following, by which the candidate with the fewest votes was declared " not " duly elected," and the election itself vacated, I dare say he would be well satisfied,

if

if they were for ever blotted out of the journals of the houfe of commons. In fair argument, no part of a precedent fhould be admitted, unlefs the whole of it be given to us together. The author has divided his precedent, for he knew, that, taken together, it produced a confequence directly the reverfe of that, which he endeavours to draw from a vote of expulfion. But what will this honeft perfon fay, if I take him at his word, and demonftrate to him, that the houfe of commons never meant to found Mr. Walpole's incapacity upon his expulfion only? What fubterfuge will then remain?

Let it be remembered that we are fpeaking of the intention of men, who lived more than half a century ago, and that fuch intention can only be collected from their words and actions, as they are delivered to us upon record. To prove their defigns by a fuppofition of what they would have done, oppofed to what they actually did, is mere trifling and impertinence. The vote, by which Mr. Walpole's incapacity was declared, is thus expreffed, " That Robert Walpole, Efq; hav-
" ing been this feffion of parliament com-
" mitted a prifoner to the Tower, and ex-
" pelled this houfe for a breach of truft in the
" execution of his office, and notorious cor-
" ruption when fecretary at war, was and is
" in-

" incapable of being elected a member to ferve
" in this prefent parliament *." Now, Sir,
to my underftanding, no propofition of this
kind can be more evident, than that the houfe
of commons, by this very vote, themfelves
underftood, and meant to declare, that Mr.
Walpole's incapacity arofe from the crimes
he had committed, not from the punifhment
the houfe annexed to them. The high breach
of truft, the notorious corruption are ftated
in the ftrongeft terms. They do not tell us
that he was incapable becaufe he was expelled,
but becaufe he had been guilty of fuch offences
as juftly rendered him unworthy of a feat in
parliament. If they had intended to fix the
difability upon his expulfion alone, the men-
tion of his crimes in the fame vote would
have been highly improper. It could only
perplex the minds of the electors, who, if
they collected any thing from fo confufed a

* A minifterial advocate has quoted this refolution unfairly, and altered it to ferve his purpofe. Mr. Dyfon,
the compiler of that tedious quarto, entitled, *The cafe of
the laft election for the county of Middlefex confidered*,
has the affurance to recite this very vote, in the following
terms, " *Refolved, that Robert Walpole, Efq; having
" been that feffion of parliament expelled the houfe, was
" and is incapable of being elected a member to ferve in
" the prefent parliament.*" There cannot be a ftronger
pofitive proof of the treachery of the compiler, nor a
ftronger prefumptive proof that he was convinced that the
vote, if truly recited, would overturn his whole argument.

dc-

declaration of the law of parliament, muſt have concluded that their repreſentative had been declared incapable becauſe he was highly guilty, not becauſe he had been puniſhed. But even admitting them to have underſtood it in the other ſenſe, they muſt then, from the very terms of the vote, have united the idea of his being ſent to the Tower with that of his expulſion, and conſidered his incapacity as the joint effect of both *.

I do not mean to give an opinion upon the juſtice of the proceedings of the houſe of commons with regard to Mr. Walpole; but certainly, if I admitted their cenſure to be well founded, I could no way avoid agreeing with them in the conſequence they drew from it. I could never have a doubt, in law or reaſon, that a man, convicted of a high breach of truſt, and of a notorious corruption, in the execution of a public office, was and ought to be incapable of ſitting in the ſame parliament. Far from attempting to invalidate that vote, I ſhould have wiſhed that the incapacity declared by it could legally have been continued for ever.

Now Sir, obſerve how forcibly the argument returns. The houſe of commons, upon

---

* See this matter farther elucidated in the letter ſigned Philo Junius, which immediately follows this.

the face of their proceedings, had the ftrong-
eſt motives to declare Mr. Walpole incapable
of being re-elected. They thought fuch a
man unworthy to fit among them :—To that
point they proceeded no farther; for they
refpected the rights of the people, while they
aſſerted their own. They did not infer, from
Mr. Walpole's incapacity, that his opponent
was duly elected ; on the contrary they declared Mr. Taylor " Not duly elected," and
the election itſelf void.

Such, however, is the precedent, which
my honeſt friend aſſures us is ſtrictly in point
to prove, that expulſion of itſelf creates an
incapacity of being elected. If it had been
fo, the prefent houfe of commons ſhould at
leaſt have followed ſtrictly the example before
them, and ſhould have ſtated to us, in the
fame vote, the crimes for which they expelled Mr. Wilkes ; whereas they refolve
fimply, that, " having been expelled, he
" was and is incapable." In this proceeding
I am authorifed to affirm, they have neither ſtatute, nor cuſtom, nor reafon, nor one
fingle precedent to fupport them. On the
other fide, there is indeed a precedent fo
ſtrongly in point, that all the inchanted
caſtles of miniſterial magic fall before it. In
the year 1698, (a period which the rankeſt
Tory dare not except againſt) Mr. Wollafton

ton was expelled, re-elected, and admitted
to take his feat in the fame parliament. The
miniftry have precluded themfelves from all
objections drawn from the caufe of his expulfion, for they affirm abfolutely, that expulfion of itfelf creates the difability. Now,
Sir, let fophiftry evade, let falfehood affert,
and impudence deny—here ftands the precedent, a land-mark to direct us through a
troubled fea of controverfy, confpicuous and
unremoved.

I HAVE dwelt the longer upon the difcuf-
fion of this point, becaufe, in my opinion,
it comprehends the whole queftion. The
reft is unworthy of notice. We are enquiring whether incapacity be or not be created
by expulfion. In the cafes of Bedford and
Malden, the incapacity of the perfons returned was matter of public notoriety, for it was
created by act of parliament. But, really,
Sir, my honeft friend's fuppofitions are as
unfavourable to him as his facts. He well
knows that the clergy, befides that they are
reprefented in common with their fellow-
fubjects, have alfo a feparate parliament of
their own :——that their incapacity to fit in
the houfe of commons has been confirmed by
repeated decifions of the houfe, and that the
law of parliament, declared by thofe decifions, has been for above two centuries notorious

rious and undifputed. The author is certainly at liberty to fancy cafes, and make
whatever comparifons he thinks proper; his
fuppofitions ftill continue as` diftant from
fact, as his wild difcourfes are from folid argument.

THE conclufion of his book is candid to
extreme. He offers to grant me all I defire.
He thinks he may fafely admit that the cafe
of Mr. Walpole makes directly againft him,
for it feems he has one grand folution *in petto*
for all difficulties. *If*, fays he, *I were to allow
all this, it will only prove, that the law of election was different in Queen Anne's time, from
what it is at prefent.*

THIS indeed is more than I expected. The
principle, I know, has been maintained in
fact, but I never expected to fee it fo formally
declared. What can he mean? Does he affume this language to fatisfy the doubts of
the people, or does he mean to roufe their indignation; are the miniftry daring enough
to affirm, that the houfe of commons have a
right to make and unmake the law of parliament at their pleafure?—Does the law
of parliament, which we are fo often told is
the law of the land;—does the common
right of every fubject of the realm depend
upon an arbitrary capricious vote of one
branch

branch of the legiflature?—The voice of truth and reafon muft be filent.

THE miniftry tell us plainly that this is no longer a queftion of right, but of power and force alone. What was law yefterday is not law to-day: and now it feems we have no better rule to live by than the temporary dif-cretion and fluctuating integrity of the houfe of commons.

PROFESSIONS of patriotifm are become ftale and ridiculous. For my own part, I claim no merit from endeavouring to do a fervice to my fellow-fubjects. I have done it to the beft of my underftanding; and, without looking for the approbation of other men, my confcience is fatisfied. What re-mains to be done concerns the collective bo-dy of the people. They are now to deter-mine for themfelves, whether they will firm-ly and conftitutionally affert their rights; or make an humble, flavifh, furrender of them at the feet of the miniftry. To a generous mind there cannot be a doubt. We owe it to our anceftors to preferve entire thefe rights, which they have delivered to our care: we owe it to our pofterity, not to fuffer their deareft inheritance to be deftroyed. But if it were poffible for us to be infenfible of thefe facred claims, there is yet an obligation bind-

ing

ing upon ourfelves, from which nothing can
acquit us,—a perfonal intereft, which we
cannot furrender. To alienate even our own
rights, would be a crime as much more enormous than fuicide, as a life of civil fecurity
and freedom is fuperior to a bare exiftence ;
and if life be the bounty of heaven, we fcorn-
fully reject the nobleft part of the gift, if we
confent to furrender that certain rule of liv-
ing, without which the condition of human
nature is not only miferable, but contemptible.

JU N I U S.

L E T T E R XXXI.

TO THE PRINTER OF THE PUBLIC
ADVERTISER.

S I R,   22 *May*, 1771.

VERY early in the debate upon the decifion of the Middlefex election, it
was obferved by Junius, that the houfe of
commons had not only exceeded their boafted precedent of the expulfion and fubfequent
incapacitation of Mr. Walpole, but that they
had not even adhered to it ftrictly as far as it
went. After convicting Mr. Dyfon of giving a falfe quotation from the Journals, and
having

having explained the purpose, which that
contemptible fraud was intended to anfwer,
he proceeds to ftate the vote itfelf, by which
Mr. Walpole's fuppofed incapacity was declared, viz.—" Refolved, That Robert Wal-
" pole, Efq; having been this feffion of par-
" liament committed a prifoner to the
" Tower, and expelled this houfe for a high
" breach of truft in the execution of his of-
" fice, and notorious corruption when fecre-
" tary at war, was and is incapable of being
" elected a member to. ferve in this prefent
" parliament :"——and then obferves that,
from the terms of the vote, we have no
right to annex the incapacitation to the expulfion only, for that, as the propofition ftands,
it muft arife equally from the expulfion and
the commitment to the Tower. I believe,
Sir, no man, who knows any thing of dia-
lectics, or who underftands Englifh, will difpute the truth and fairnefs of this conftruction. But Junius has a great authority to
fupport him, which, to fpeak with the Duke
of Grafton, I accidentally met with this
morning in the courfe of my reading. It
contains an admonition, which cannot be
repeated too often. Lord Sommers, in his
excellent tract upon the rights of the people,
after reciting the votes of the convention of
the 28th of January 1689, viz.—" that King
" James the fecond, having endeavoured to
" fub-

" fubvert the conftitution of this kingdom
" by breaking the original contract between
" King and people, and by the advice of
" jefuits and other wicked perfons having
" violated the fundamental laws, and having
" withdrawn himfelf out of this kingdom,
" hath abdicated the government, &c."——
makes this obfervation upon it. " The
" word abdicated relates to all the claufes
" aforegoing, as well as to his deferting the
" kingdom, or elfe they would have been
" wholly in vain." And that there might
be no pretence for confining the abdication
merely to the withdrawing, Lord Sommers
farther obferves, *that King James, by refufing
to govern us according to that law, by which he
held the crown, implicitly renounced his title to
it.*

IF Junius's conftruction of the vote againft
Mr. Walpole be now admitted, (and indeed
I cannot comprehend how it can honeftly be
difputed) the advocates of the houfe of commons muft either give up their precedent entirely, or be reduced to the neceffity of maintaining one of the groffeft abfurdities ima-
ginable, viz. " That a commitment to the
" Tower is a conftituent part of, and contri-
" butes half at leaft to the incapacitation of
" the perfon who fuffers it."

I NEED

I NEED not make you any excuse for endeavouring to keep alive the attention of the public to the decision of the Middlesex election. The more I consider it, the more I am convinced that, as a fact, it is indeed highly injurious to the rights of the people; but that, as a precedent, it is one of the most dangerous that ever was established against those who are to come after us. Yet I am so far a moderate man, that I verily believe the majority of the house of commons, when they passed this dangerous vote, neither understood the question, nor knew the consequence of what they were doing. Their motives were rather despicable, than criminal, in the extreme. One effect they certainly did not foresee. They are now reduced to such a situation, that if a member of the present house of commons were to conduct himself ever so improperly, and in reality deserve to be sent back to his constituents with a mark of disgrace, they would not dare to expel him; because they know that the people, in order to try again the great question of right, or to thwart an odious house of commons, would probably overlook his immediate unworthiness, and return the same person to parliament,—But, in time, the precedent will gain strength. A future house of commons will have no such apprehensions, consequently will not scruple to follow a pre-

cedent,

tedent, which they did not eftablifh. The
Mifer himfelf feldom lives to enjoy.the fruit
of his extortion; but his heir fucceeds him
of courfe, and takes poffeffion without cenfure. No man expects him to make reftitu-
tion, and, no matter for his title, he lives
quietly upon the eftate.

PHILO JUNIUS.

LETTER XXXIII.

TO THE PRINTER OF THE PUBLIC
ADVERTISER.

SIR,   22 Auguſt, 1769.

I MUST beg of you to print a few lines,
in explanation of fome paffages in my
laft letter, which I fee have been mifunder-
ftood.

1. WHEN I faid, that the houfe of commons never meant to found Mr. Walpole's
incapacity on this expulfion only, I meant no
more than to deny the general propofition,
that expulfion alone creates the incapacity.
If there be any thing ambiguous in the expreffion, I beg leave to explain it by faying,
that, in my opinion, expulfion neither cre-

I 2   ates,

ates, nor in any part contributes to create the incapacity in queftion.

2. I CAREFULLY avoided entering into the merits of Mr. Walpole's cafe. I did not enquire, whether the houfe of commons acted juftly, or whether they truly declared the law of parliament. My remarks went only to their apparent meaning and intention, as it ftands declared in their own refolution.

3. I NEVER meant to affirm, that a commitment to the Tower created a difqualification. On the contrary, I confidered that idea as an abfurdity, into which the miniftry muft inevitably fall, if they reafoned right upon their own principles.

THE cafe of Mr. Wollafton fpeaks for itfelf. The miniftry affert that *expulfion alone* creates an abfolute, complete incapacity to be re-elected to fit in the fame parliament. This propofition they have uniformly maintained, without any condition or modification whatfoever. Mr. Wollafton was expelled, re-elected, and admitted to take his feat in the fame parliament.—I leave it to the public to determine, whether this be a plain matter of fact, or mere nonfenfe or declamation.

JUNIUS.

LETTER

LETTER XXXIV.

TO THE PRINTER OF THE PUBLIC AD-
VERTISER.

4 *Sept,* 1769.

ARGUMENT againſt FACT; or, A new
fyſtem of political Logic, by which the
miniſtry have demonſtrated, to the ſatiſ-
faction of their friends, that expulſion
alone creates a complete incapacity to be
re-elected: *alias,* that a ſubject of this realm
may be robbed of his common right, by a
vote of the houſe of commons....

FIRST FACT.

MR. *Wollaſton, in* 1698, *was expelled, re-
elected, and admitted to take his ſeat,...*

ARGUMENT.

As this cannot conveniently be reconciled with our general propoſition, it may be
neceſſary to ſhift our ground, and look back
to the *cauſe* of Mr. Wollaſton's expulſion.
From thence it will appear clearly that, " al-
" though he was expelled, he had not ren-
" dered himſelf a culprit too ignominious to
" fit in parliament, and that having reſigned
I 3   " his

" his employment, he was no longer inca-
" pacitated by law." *Vide Serious Considera-*
tions, page 23. Or thus, " The house,
" somewhat *inaccurately,* used the word EX-
" PELLED ; they should have called it A.MO-
" TION." *Vide Mungo's case confidered, page*
11. Or in short, if these arguments should
be thought insufficient, we may fairly deny
the fact. For example ; " I affirm that he
" was not re-elected. The same Mr. Wol-
" lafton, who was expelled, was not again
" elected. The same individual, if you
" please, walked into the house, and took his
" feat there, but the same perfon in law was
" not admitted a member of that parliament,
" from which he had been difcarded." *Vide*
Letter to Junius, page 12.

SECOND FACT.

Mr. Walpole having been committed to the
Tower, and expelled for a high breach of truft
and notorious corruption in a public office, was
declared incapable, &c.

ARGUMENT.

From the terms of this vote, nothing can
be more evident than that the house of commons meant to fix the incapacity upon the
punifhment, and not upon the crime ; but
left it fhould appear in a different light to
weak, uninformed perfons, it may be advife-
able

able to gut the refolution, and give it to the
public, with all poffible folemnity, in the
following terms, viz. " Refolved, that Ro-
" bert Walpole, Efq; having been that fef-
" fion of parliament expelled the houfe, was
" and is incapable of being elected member
" to ferve in that prefent parliament." *Vide
Mungo on the ufe of quotations, page* 11.

N. B. THE author of the anfwer to Sir
William Meredith feems to have made ufe of
Mungo's quotation, for in page 18, he affures
us, " That the declaratory vote of the 17th
" of February, 1769, was indeed a literal
" copy of the refolution of the houfe in Mr.
" Walpole's cafe."

THIRD FACT.

*His opponent, Mr. Taylor, having the fmall-
eft number of votes at the next election, was declared* NOT DULY ELECTED.

ARGUMENT.

THIS fact we confider as directly in point
to prove that Mr. Luttrell ought to be the
fitting member, for the following reafons.
" The burgeffes of Lynn could draw no
" other inference from this refolution, but
" this, that at a future election, and in cafe
" of a fimilar return, the houfe would re-
" ceive the fame candidate as duly elected,

" whom

" whom they had before rejected." *Vide Poſt-*
ſcript to Junius, p. 37. Or thus : " This
" their reſolution leaves no room to doubt,
" what part they *would* have taken, if, upon
" a ſubſequent re-election of Mr. Walpole,
" there had been any other candidate in com-
" petition, with him. For, by their vote,
" they could have no other intention than to
" admit ſuch other candidate." *Vide Mun-*
go's caſe conſidered, p. 39. Or take it in this
light.—The burgeſſes of Lynn having, in
defiance of the houſe, retorted upon them
a perſon, whom they had branded with the
moſt ignominious marks of their diſpleaſure,
were thereby ſo well intitled to favour and
indulgence, that the houſe could do no leſs
than rob Mr. Taylor of a right legally veſted
in him, in order that the burgeſſes might be
appriſed of the law of parliament ; which
law, the houſe took a very direct way of ex-
plaining to them, by reſolving that the candidate with the feweſt votes was not duly
elected :—" And was not this much more
" equitable, more in the ſpirit of that equal
" and ſubſtantial juſtice, which is the end of
" all law, than if they had violently adhered
" to the ſtrict maxims of law ?". *Vide Serious*
Conſiderations, p. 33 and 34. " And if the
" preſent houſe of commons had choſen to
" follow the ſpirit of this reſolution, they
" would have received and eſtabliſhed the
" can-

" candidate with the feweſt votes." *Vide An-*
ſwer to Sir William Meredith, p. 18.

PERMIT me now, Sir, to ſhew you that
the worthy Dr. Blackſtone ſometimes contradicts the miniſtry as well as himſelf. The
Speech without doors aſſerts, page 9, " that
" the legal effect of an incapacity, founded
" on a judicial determination of a complete
" court, is preciſely the ſame as that of an
" incapacity created by act of parliament."
Now for the Doctor—*The law and the opi-*
nion of the judge are not always convertible terms,
or one and the ſame thing ; ſince it ſometimes may
happen that the judge may miſtake the law.
Commentaries, Vol. I. p. 71.

THE anſwer to Sir William Meredith aſſerts, page 23, " That the returning of-
" ficer is not a judicial, but a purely mi-
" niſterial officer. His return is no judicial
" act."—At 'em again Doctor. *The Sheriff,*
in his judicial capacity, is to hear and determine
cauſes of 40 ſhillings value and under in his
county court. He has alſo a judicial power in di-
vers other civil caſes. He is likewiſe to decide the
elections of knights of the ſhire (ſubject to the
control of the houſe of commons), to judge of
the qualification of voters, and to return ſuch as
he ſhall DETERMINE *to be duly elected.* Vide
Commentaries, page 332. Vol. I.

WHAT

WHAT conclusion shall we draw from such facts, and such arguments, such contradictions? I cannot express my opinion of the present ministry more exactly than in the words of Sir Richard Steele, " *that we are* " *governed by a set of drivellers, whose folly* " *takes away all dignity from distress, and makes* " *even calamity ridiculous.*"

PHILO JUNIUS.

The following curious letter is omitted in the author's own edition. The double entendre though very delicately carried forward, was perhaps thought an improper subject to be classed with grave political matter.

LETTER XXXV.

TO THE PRINTER OF THE PUBLIC ADVERTISER.

SIR,

I FIND myself unexpectedly married in the newspapers, without my knowledge or consent. Since I am fated to be a husband, I hope at least the lady will perform the principal duty of a wife. Marriages, they
say,

fay, are made in heaven, but they are con-
fummated. upon earth; and since Junia* has
adopted my name, fhe cannot, in common
matrimonial decency, refufe to make me a
tender of her perfon. Politics are too bar-
ren a fubject for a new-married couple. I
fhould be glad to furnifh her with one more
fit for a lady to handle, and better fuited to
the natural dexterity of her fex. In fhort, if
Junia be young and handfome, fhe will have
no reafon to complain of my method of conducting an argument. I abominate all ter-
giverfation in difcourfe, *and fhe may be affured
that whatever I advance, whether it be weak
or forcible, fhall, at at any rate, be directly in
point.* It is true I am a ftrenuous advocate
for liberty and property, but when thefe
rights are invaded by a pretty woman, I am
neither able to defend my money nor my
freedom. The divine right of beauty is the
only one an Englifhman ought to acknowledge, and a pretty woman the only tyrant
he is not authorifed to refift.

J U N I U S.

* The fignature of a letter in the papers.

16   LETTER

LETTER XXXVI.

TO HIS GRACE THE DUKE OF BEDFORD.

MY LORD, 19 Sept. 1769.

YOU are fo little accuftomed to receive
any marks of refpect or efteem from
the public, that, if in the following lines,
a compliment or expreffion of applaufe
fhould efcape me, I fear you would confider
it as a mockery of your eftablifhed character,
and perhaps an infult to your underftanding.
You have nice feelings, my Lord, if we may
judge from your refentments. Cautious therefore of giving offence, where you have fo little
deferved it, I fhall leave the illuftration of
your virtues to other hands. Your friends
have a privilege to play upon the eafinefs of
your temper, or poffibly they are better acquainted with your good qualities than I am.
You have done good by ftealth. The reft is
upon record. You have ftill left ample room
for fpeculation, when panegyric is exhaufted.

You are indeed a very confiderable man.
The higheft rank ;—a fplendid fortune ;
and a name glorious till it was yours, were
fufficient to have fupported you with meaner
abilities

abilities than I think you poffefs. From the firft, you derive a conftitutional claim to re-fpect; from the fecond, a natural extenfive authority;—the laft created a partial expectation, of hereditary virtues. The ufe you, have made of thefe uncommon advantages might have been more honourable to yourfelf, but could not be more inftructive to mankind. We may trace it in the veneration of your country, the choice of your friends, and in the accomplifhment of every fanguine hope, which the public might have conceived from the illuftrious name of Ruffel.

THE eminence of your ftation gave you a commanding profpect of your duty. The road, which led to honour, was open to your view. You could not lofe it by miftake, and you had no temptation to depart from it by defign. Compare the natural dignity, and importance of the richeft peer of England;—the noble independence, which he might have maintained in parliament, and the real intereft and refpect, which he might have acquired, not only in parliament, but through the whole kingdom; compare thefe glorious diftinctions, with the ambition, of holding a fhare in government, the emoluments of a place, the fale of a borough, or the purchafe of a corporation; and though you may not regret the virtues, which create refpect, respect, you may see with anguish, how much real importance and authority you have lost. Consider the character of an independent, virtuous Duke of Bedford; imagine what he might be in this country, then reflect one moment upon what you are. If it be possible for me to withdraw my attention from the fact, I will tell you in theory what such a man might be.

Conscious of his own weight and importance, his conduct in parliament would be directed by nothing but the constitutional duty of a peer. He would consider himself as a guardian of the laws. Willing to support the just measures of government, but determined to observe the conduct of the minister with suspicion, he would oppose the violence of faction with as much firmness, as the encroachments of prerogative. He would be as little capable of bargaining with the minister for places for himself, or his dependants, as of descending to mix himself in the intrigues of opposition. Whenever an important question called for his opinion in parliament, he would be heard, by the most profligate minister, with deference and respect. His authority would either sanctify or disgrace the measures of government.—The people would look up to him as to their protector, and a virtuous prince would have one honest

honeſt man in his dominions, in whoſe integrity and judgment he might ſafely con-
fide. If it ſhould be the will of providence
to afflict him with a domeſtic misfortune*, he
would ſubmit to the ſtroke, with feeling,
but not without dignity. He would conſider
the people as his children, and receive a generous heart-felt conſolation, in the ſympa-
thiſing tears, and bleſſings of his country.

Your Grace may probably diſcover ſomething more intelligible in the negative part of
this illuſtrious character. The man' I have
deſcribed would never proſtitute his dignity'
in parliament by an indecent violence either
in oppoſing or defending a miniſter. He
would not at one moment rancorouſly perſe-

---

* The Duke had lately loſt his only ſon, Francis
Marquis of Taviſtock. The horſe of this amiable young
nobleman fell under him in leaping a low hedge as he
was returning from a fox chaſe, and in ſtruggling to
riſe trampled on the Marquis's head, and fractured his
ſkull. The Marquis died of the wound, March 22d,
1767, univerſally lamented. He was in the 28th year
of his age. His excellent conſort, Elizabeth, the
daughter of William Anne, Earl of Albemarle, and
ſiſter to the preſent Admiral Keppel, being inconſolable
for her loſs, languiſhed about a year and an half, and
died Nov. 2d, 1768. At her death, ſhe was alſo in the
28th year of her age. The Marquis had two ſons by
this lady; the eldeſt, Francis, now Duke of Bedford,
was born Aug. 11, 1765.

cute

cute, at another basely cringe to the favourite
of his Sovereign. After outraging the royal
dignity with, peremptory conditions, little
short of menace and hostility, he would never descend to the humility of soliciting an
interview * with the favourite, and of offer-
ing to recover, at any price, the honour of
his friendship. Though deceived perhaps in
his youth, he would not, through the course
of a long life, have invariably chosen his
friends from among the most profligate of
mankind. His own honour would have forbidden him from mixing his private pleasures
or conversation with jockeys, gamesters,
blasphemers, gladiators, or buffoons. He
would then have never felt, much less would
he have submitted to the dishonest necessity
of engaging in the interests and intrigues of
his dependents, of supplying their vices, or
relieving their beggary, at the expence of his
country. He would not have betrayed such
ignorance, or such contempt of the constitution, as openly to avow, in a court of justice,
the † purchase and sale of a borough. He

---

* It is said the Duke solicited this interview. The parties met at the late Earl of Eglingtouns, but Lord Bute
declared to the Duke, that he would never have any more
connexion with a man who had already betrayed him.

† His Grace, for a certain sum, had promised to return a gentleman to parliament for one of his Boroughs. A suit was brought against him for the recovery of the money, and he was obliged to repay it.

would

would not have thought it confiftent with
his rank in the ftate, or even with his perfonal importance, to be the little tyrant of a
little corporation †. He would never have
been infulted with virtues, which he had la-
boured to extinguifh, nor fuffered the difgrace of a mortifying defeat, which has made
him ridiculous and contemptible, even to the
few by whom he was not detefted.—I reve-
rence the afflictions of a good man,—his for-
rows are facred. But how can we take part in
the diftreffes of a man, whom we can neither
love nor efteem; or feel for a calamity, of
which he himfelf is infenfible? Where was
the father's heart, when he could look for,
or find an immediate confolation for the lofs
of an only fon, in confultations and bargains
for a place at court, and even in the mifery
of balloting at the India Houfe!

ADMITTING then that you have miftaken
or deferted thofe honourable principles, which
ought to have directed your conduct; admitting that you have as little claim to private
affection as to public efteem, let us fee with

---

† THE Corporation of Bedford entertained fuch a
diflike to his affumed patronage, that they admitted a
number of ftrangers to the freedom of that town, and
totally fhook off his Grace. The public cannot have
forgot the excurfions of numbers of people from London, in order to be made free of that corporation.

what abilities, with what degree of judgment
you have carried your own fyftem into execution. A great man, in the fuccefs and even
in the magnitude of his crimes, finds a refcue from contempt. Your Grace is every
way unfortunate. Yet I will not look back
to thofe ridiculous fcenes; by which in your
earlier days, you thought it an honour to be
diftinguifhed,* ;—the recorded ftripes, the
public infamy, your own fufferings, or Mr.
Rigby's fortitude. Thefe events undoubtedly left an impreffion, though not upon your
mind. To fuch a mind, it may perhaps be a
pleafure to reflect, that there is hardly a corner of any of his Majefty's kingdoms, ex-

* MR. HUMPHREYS, an Attorney, attacked his
Grace with his horfewhip at Litchfield Races with great
feverity. He was refcued by the vigour and intrepidity
of Mr. Rigby. This was a dangerous fervice, for Mr.
Humphreys was ftrongly fupported. This generous interpofition occafioned the after clofe connection between his Grace and Mr. Rigby. The following ftrcke
of Lord Chefterfield has greatly affifted to keep alive
his Grace's Litchfield adventure. Sir Edward Hawke,
in his official letter, after defeating the French Fleet in
1747, faid, that the French fhips being large took a
great deal of DRUBBING ; his Majefty not underftanding the word, afked Lord Chefterfield to explain it ;
but his Lordfhip feeing the Duke of Bedford, at that
inftant, enter the clofet, referred the King to his Grace,
as a nobleman much more able to do it, from having
felt it experimentally.

cept France, in which, at one time or other, your valuable life has not been in danger: Amiable man! we fee and acknowledge the protection of Providence, by which you have fo often efcaped the perfonal deteftation of your fellow fubjects, and are ftill referved for the public juftice of your country.

Your hiftory begins to be important at that aufpicious period, at which you were de-, puted to reprefent the Earl of Bute, at the court of Verfailles. It was an honourable office, and executed with the fame fpirit, with which it was accepted. Your patrons want- ed an ambaffador, who would. fubmit to make conceffions, without daring to infift upon any honourable condition for his So- vereign. Their bufinefs required a man, who had as little feeling for his own dignity as for the welfare of his country; and they found him in the firft rank of the nobility. Belleifle, Goree, Guadeloupe, St. Lucia, Martinique, the Fifhery, and the Havannah, are glorious monuments of your Grace's ta- lents for negociation. My Lord, we are too well acquainted with your pecuniary character, to think it poffible that fo many public facrifices fhould have been made, with- out fome private compenfations. Your con- duct carries with it an internal evidence, be- yond all the legal proofs of a court of juftice.

Even

Even the callous pride of Lord Egremont *
was alarmed. He faw and felt his own difhonour in correfponding with you; and there
certainly was a moment, at which he meant
to have refifted, had not a fatal lethargy prevailed over his faculties, and carried all fenfe
and memory away with it.

I will not pretend to fpecify the fecret
terms on which you were invited to fupport
an adminiftration † which Lord Bute pretended to leave in full poffeffion of their minifterial authority, and perfectly mafters of
themfelves. He was not of a temper to relin-
quifh power, though he retired from employment. Stipulations were certainly made
between your Grace and him, and certainly
violated. After two years fubmiffion, you
thought you had collected a ftrength fufficient to controul his influence, and that it was
your turn to be a tyrant, becaufe you had
been a flave. When you found yourfelf miftaken in your opinion of your gracious Mafter's firmnefs, difappointment got the better

---

* THE Earl of Egremont, when his Grace was
negociating the Peace of Paris, wrote a letter to him,
which gave fuch offence, that the Duke wrote to be
recalled. It has been faid, that it coft Lord Bute fome
trouble to pacify him.

† THE Grenville Adminiftration.

of

of all your humble difcretion, and carried
you to an excefs of outrage to his perfon ‡, as
diftant from true fpirit, as from all decency
and refpeĉt. After robbing him of the
rights of a King, you would not permit him
to preferve the honour of a gentleman. It
was then Lord Weymouth was nominated
to Ireland, and difpatched (we well remember with what indecent hurry) to plunder
the treafury of the firft fruits of an employment which you well knew he was never to
execute ‖.

THIS fudden declaration of war againft
the favourite might have given you a momentary merit with the public, if it had
either been adopted upon principle, or maintained with refolution. Without looking back
to all your former fervility, we need only ob-

‡ WHEN Mr. Grenville attempted to exclude the
Princefs Dowager out of the Regency, his difmiffion
was determined upon. When the Duke was informed
of this, he afked an audience of a certain perfon, re-
proached him in the groffeft manner, and it was declared, fhocked his fenfibility to fuch a degree, as to
leave him in convulfions.

‖ LORD WEYMOUTH did not go to Ireland, but
he received three thoufand pounds for plate and equi-
page, which are always iffued as foon as the appointment is made.

ferve

ferve your fubfequent conduct, to fee upon
what motives you acted. Apparently united
with Mr. Grenville, you waited until Lord
Rockingham's feeble adminiftration fhould
diffolve in its own weaknefs.—The moment
their difmiffion was fufpected, the moment
you perceived that another fyftem was adopted
in the clofet, you thought it no difgrace to
return to your former dependance, and folicit
once more the friendfhip of Lord Bute. You
begged an interview, at which he had fpirit
enough to treat you with contempt.

It would now be of little ufe to point out,
by what a train of weak, injudicious meafures,
it became neceffary, or was thought fo, to call
you back to a fhare in the adminiftration.
The friends, whom you did not in the laft
inftance defert, were not of a character to add
ftrength or credit to government; and at that
time your alliance with the Duke of Grafton
was, I prefume, hardly forefeen. We muft
look for other ftipulations, to account for that
fudden refolution of the clofet, by which three
of your dependants * (whofe characters, I
think, cannot be lefs refpected than they are)

* Lord Gower, Vifcount Weymouth, and Earl
of Sandwich. Lord Gower is now the head of the
Bedford party. Lord Sandwich fet up for himfelf after
the death of the Duke. Witnefs Lord Gower's fupport
of Admiral Keppel againft Lord Sandwich.

were

were advanced to offices, through which you might again controul the minifter, and probably engrofs the whole direction of affairs.

THE poffeffion of abfolute power is now once more within your reach. The meafures you have taken to obtain and confirm it, are too grofs to efcape the eyes of a difcerning judicious prince. His palace is befieged; the lines of circumvallation are drawing round him; and unlefs he finds a refource in his own activity, or in the attachment of the real friends of his family, the beft of princes muft fubmit to the confinement of a ftate prifoner, until your Grace's death, or fome lefs fortunate event fhall raife the fiege. For the prefent, you may fafely refume that ftile of infult and menace, which even a private gentleman cannot fubmit to hear without being contemptible. Mr. Mackenzie's hiftory is not yet forgotten, and you may find precedents enough of the mode, in which an imperious fubject may fignify his pleafure to his Sovereign. Where will this gracious monarch look for affiftance, when the wretched Grafton could forget his obligations to his mafter, and defert him for a hollow alliance with *fuch* a man as the Duke of Bedford.

LET us confider you, then, as arrived at the fummit of worldly greatnefs: let us fuppofe,

pofe, that all your plans of avarice and ambition are accomplifhed, and your moſt ſan-
guine wifhes gratified in the fear, as well as
the hatred of the people : Can age itſelf forget that you are now, in the laſt act of life?
Can grey hairs make folly venerable? and is
there no period to be reſerved for meditation
and retirement? For fhame! my Lord:
let it not be recorded of you, that the lateſt
moments of your life were dedicated to the
ſame unworthy purſuits, the ſame buſy agi-
tations, in which your youth and manhood
were exhauſted. Conſider, that, although
you cannot diſgrace your former life, you are
violating the character of age, and expoſing
the impotent imbecility, after you have loſt
the vigour of the paſſions.

YOUR friends will aſk, perhaps, Whither
fhall this unhappy old man retire? Can he
remain in the metropolis, where his life has
been ſo often threatened, and his palace ſo
often attacked? If he returns to Wooburn*,
ſcorn and mockery await him. He muſt create
a ſolitude round his eſtate, if he would avoid
the face of reproach and deriſion. At Ply-
mouth, his deſtruction would be more than
probable; at Exeter, inevitable. No honeſt
Englifhman will ever forget his attachment,

* THE Duke's ſeat in Bedfordſhire.

nor

nor any honeſt Scotchman forgive his treachery
to Lord Bute. At every town he enters, he
muſt change his liveries and name. Which
ever way he flies, the *Hue and Cry* of the
country purſues him.

In another kingdom indeed, the bleſſings
of his adminiſtration have been more ſenſibly
felt; his virtues better underſtood; or at
worſt, they will not, for him alone, forget
their hoſpitality.—As well might VERRES
have returned to Italy. You have twice
eſcaped, my Lord: beware of a third experiment. The indignation of a whole people,
plundered, inſulted, and oppreſſed as they have
been, will not be always diſappointed.

It is in vain therefore to ſhift the ſcene.
You can no more fly from your enemies than
from yourſelf. Perſecuted abroad, you look
into your own heart for conſolation, and find
nothing but reproaches and deſpair. But,
my Lord, you may quit the field of buſineſs, though not the field of danger; and
though you cannot be ſafe, you may ceaſe
to be ridiculous. I fear you have liſtened
too long to the advice of thoſe pernicious
friends, with whoſe intereſts you have ſor-
didly united your own, and for whom you
have ſacrificed every thing that ought to be
dear to a man of honour. They are ſtill

bafe enough to encourage the follies of your
age, as they once did the vices of your
youth. As little acquainted with the rules
of decorum, as with the laws of morality,
they will not fuffer you to profit by experience, nor even to confult the propriety of
a bad character. Even now they tell you,
that life is no more than a dramatic fcene,
in which the hero fhould preferve his confiftency to the laft, and that as you lived
without virtue, you fhould die * without repentance.

JUNIUS.

* His Grace furvived the publication of this letter
about fourteen months. He died, January 15th, 1771,
in the 61ft year of his age, at his houfe in Bloomfbury
Square.

LETTER.

L E T T E R XXXVII.

SIR WILLIAM DRAPER * TO JUNIUS.

S I R, 14 *September*, 1769.

HAVING accidentally feen a *republica-tion* of your letters, wherein you have been pleafed to *affert*, that I had fold the companions of my fuccefs; I am again ob-liged to declare the faid affertion to be a moft *infamous* and *malicious falfehood*; and I *again* call upon you to ftand forth, avow yourfelf, and *prove* the charge. If you can make it out to the fatisfaction of any one man in the kingdom, I will be content to be thought the worft man in it; if you do not, what muft the nation think of you? *Party* has nothing to do in this affair: you have made a perfonal attack upon my honour, defamed me by a moft vile calumny, which might poffibly have funk into oblivion, had not fuch uncommon

---

* SIR WILLIAM DRAPER, having been ftopped in his career of writing in defence of the Marquis of Granby, by the Marquis himfelf, in the above letter, opens the conteft on his own account. Junius by the motto to his reply, feems to hint, and very juftly, that his former animadverfions continued to rankle in Sir William's mind.

K 2 paint

pains been taken to renew and perpetuate this
scandal, chiefly because it has been told in
good language : for I give you full credit for
your elegant diction, well turned periods, and
attic wit ; but wit is oftentimes false, though
it may appear brilliant ; which is exactly the
case of your *whole performance.* But, Sir, I
am obliged in the most *serious* manner to accuse you of being guilty of *falsities.* You have
said the thing that is *not.* To support your
story, you have recourse to the following *irre-
sistible* argument : " You *sold* the companions
" of your victory, because when the 16th regi-
" ment was given to *you,* you was *silent.*" The
conclusion is inevitable. I believe that such
deep and *acute reasoning* could only come from
such an extraordinary writer as *Junius.* But
unfortunately for you, the *premises* as well as
the *conclusion* are absolutely *false.* Many applications have been made to the ministry on the
subject of the Manilla Ransom *since* the time
of my being colonel of that regiment. As I
have for some years quitted London, I was
obliged to have recourse to the honourable
Colonel Monson and Sir Samuel Cornish to
negotiate for me ; in the last autumn, I per-
sonally delivered a memorial to the Earl of
Shelburne at his seat in Wiltshire. As you
have told us of your importance, that you are
a person of *rank* and *fortune,* and above a
common bribe, you may in all probability be
not

not *unknown* to his lordſhip, who can ſatisfy you of the truth of what I ſay. But I ſhall now take the liberty, Sir, to ſeize your battery, and turn it againſt yourſelf. If your puerile and tinſel logic could carry the leaſt weight or conviction with it, how muſt you ſtand affected by the *inevitable concluſion*, as you are pleaſed to term it? According to *Junius, Silence* is *Guilt*. In many of the public papers, you have been called in the moſt direct and offenſive terms a *liar* and a *coward*. When did you reply to theſe foul accuſations? You have been quite *ſilent*; quite chop-fallen : therefore *becauſe* you was *ſilent*, the nation has a right to pronounce you to be both a liar and a coward from your own argument : but, Sir, I will give you fair play ; will afford you an opportunity to wipe off the firſt appellation ; by deſiring the proofs of your charge againſt me. Produce them ! To wipe off the laſt, produce *yourſelf*. People cannot bear any longer your *Lion's ſkin*, and the deſpicable *impoſture* of the *old Roman name* which you have *affected*. For the future aſſume the name of ſome *modern* * bravo and dark aſſaſſin : let your appellation have ſome affinity to your practice. But if I muſt *periſh*,

---

* FROM the above expreſſion, one would imagine that Sir William thought Brutus an *ancient* bravo and dark aſſaſſin.

Junias, let me *perish* in the face of day; be
for *once* a generous and open enemy.   I allow
that gothic *appeals* to cold iron are no better
proofs of a man's honesty and veracity than
hot iron and burning ploughshares are of
female chastity: but a soldier's honour is as
delicate as a woman's; it must not be suf-
pected; you have dared to throw more than
a suspicion upon mine: you cannot but know
the consequences, which even the meekness
of Christianity would pardon me for, after
the injury you have done me.

WILLIAM DRAPER,

LETTER XXXVIII.

Hæret lateri lethalis arundo.

TO SIR WILLIAM DRAPER, K. B.

SIR,   *25 September,* 1769.

AFTER so long an interval, I did not
expect to see the debate revived between us.   My answer to your last letter shall
be short; for I write to you with reluctance,
and I hope we shall now conclude our cor-
respondence for ever.

HAD

HAD you been originally and without provocation attacked by an anonymous writer, you would have had fome right to demand his name. But in this caufe you are a volunteer. You engaged in it with the unpremeditated gallantry of a foldier. You were content to fet your name in oppofition to a man, who would probably continue in conccalment. You underftood the terms upon which we were to correfpond, and gave at leaft a tacit affent to them. After voluntarily attacking me under the character of Junius, what poffible right have you to know me under any other? Will you forgive me if I infinuate to you, that you forefaw fome honour in the apparent fpirit of coming forward in perfon, and that you were not quite indifferent to the difplay of your literary qualifications?

You cannot but know that the republication of my letters was no more than a catchpenny contrivance of a printer, in which it was impoffible I fhould be concerned, and for which I am no way anfwerable. At the fame time I wifh you to underftand, that if I do not take the trouble of reprinting thefe papers, it is not from any fear of giving offence to Sir William Draper.

Your remarks upon a fignature, adopted merely for diftinction, are unworthy of no

tice ; but when you tell me I have fubmitted
to be called a liar and a coward, I muft afk
you in my turn, whether you ferioufly think it
any wȧy incumbent upon me to take notice
of the filly invectives of every fimpleton, who
writes in a news-paper ; and what opinion
you would have conceived of my difcretion,
if I had fuffered myfelf to be the dupe of fo
fhallow an artifice ?

Your appeal to the fword, though confiftent enough with your late profeffion, will
neither prove your innocence nor clear you
from   fufpicion.——Your   complaints with
regard to the Manilla ranfom were, for a confiderable time, a diftrefs to government. You
were appointed (greatly out of your turn) to
the command of a regiment, and *during that
adminiftration* we heard no more of Sir William Draper.   The facts, of which I fpeak,
may indeed be varioufly accounted for, but
they are too notorious to be denied ; and I
.think you might have learnt at the univerfity,
that a falfe conclufion is an error in argument, not a breach of veracity.   Your foli-
citaticn?, I doubt not, were renewed under
another adminiftration.   Admitting the fact,
I fear an indifferent perfon would only infer
from it, that experience had made you acquainted with the benefits of complaining.
Remember, Sir, that you have yourfelf con-
feffed

fefled, that, *confidering the critical fituation of
this country, the miniftry are in the right to tem-
porife with Spain.* This confeflion reduces
you to an unfortunate dilemma. By renew-
ing your folicitations, you muft either mean
to force your country into a war at a moft
unfeafonable juncture; or, having no view or
expectation of that kind, that you look for nothing but a private compenfation to yourfelf.

As to me, it is by no means neceffary that
I fhould be expofed to the refentment of the
worft and the moft powerful men in this
country, though I may be indifferent about
yours. Though *you* would fight, there are
others who would affaffinate.

But after all, Sir, where is the injury?
You affure me, that my logic is puerile and
tinfel, that it carries not the leaft weight or
conviction, that my premifes are falfe and my
conclufions abfurd. If this be a juft defcription of me, how is it poffible for fuch a writer
to difturb your peace of mind, or to injure a
character fo well eftablifhed as yours? Take
care, Sir William, how you indulge this unruly temper, left the world fhould fufpect that
confcience has fome fhare in your refentments. You have more to fear from the
treachery of your own paffions, than from
any malevolence of mine.

K 5
I BE-

I BELIEVE, Sir, you will never know me.. A confiderable time muft certainly elapfe before we are perfonally acquainted. You need not, however, regret the delay, or fuffer an apprehenfion that any length of time can reftore you to the Chriftian meeknefs of your temper, and difappoint your prefent indignation. If I underftand your charaċter, there, is in your own breaft a repofitory, in which your refentments may be fafely laid up for future occafions, and, preferved without the hazard of diminution. The *Odia in longum jaciens, quæ reconderet, auċtaque promeret*, I thought had only belonged to the worft character of antiquity. The text is in Tacitus.; —you know beft where to look for the commentary.

JUNIUS.

· LETTER

LETTER XXXIX.

FROM SIR WILLIAM DRAPER. A WORD AT PARTING TO JUNIUS *.

S I R,   7 *October*, 1769.

A S you have not favoured me with either of the *explanations* demanded of
you, I can have nothing more to fay to you
upon my *own* account. Your mercy to
me, or tendernefs for yourfelf, has been very
great. The public will judge of your *motives*. If your excefs of modefty forbids you
to produce either the proofs or yourfelf, I
will excufe it. Take courage, I have not
the temper of Tiberius, any more than the
rank or power. You, indeed, are a tyrant of
another fort, and upon your political bed of
torture can excruciate any fubject, from a
firft minifter down to fuch a grub or butter-
fly as myfelf; like another detefted tyrant of
antiquity, can make the wretched fufferer fit

---

* SIR WILLIAM was on the eve of his departure to
the continent of Britifh America. Junius had the honour
of fending him on his travels. Four days after the
date of this letter he agreed with a Briftol Trader, for.
his paffage to South Carolina.

the

the bed, if the bed will not fit the fufferer,
by disjointing or tearing the trembling limbs
until they are ftretched to its extremity.   But
courage, conftancy, and patience, under tor-
ments, have fometimes caufed the moft hard-
ened monfters to relent, and forgive the object of their cruelty.   You, Sir, are determined to try all that human nature can en-
dure, until fhe expires : elfe, was it poffible
that you could be the author of that moft in-
human letter to the Duke of Bedford, I have
read with aftonifhment and horror? Where,
Sir, where were the feelings of your own
heart, when you could upbraid a moft affec-
tionate father with the lofs of his only and
moft amiable fon? Read over again thofe
cruel lines of yours, and let them wring
your very foul! Cannot political queftions
be difcuffed without defcending to the moft
odious perfonalities?* Muft you go wantonly

out

---

* MODERN degeneracy is not to be touched or reformed by meek cenfures. Political as well as moral
offenders muft fmart under the lafh. Mr. Pope, in his
letter, dated July 26th, 1734, to Dr. Arbuthnot, fays,
with truth on his fide, that " To reform and not to
" chaftife, I am afraid, is impoffible; and that the
" beft precepts, as well as the beft laws, would prove
" of fmall ufe, if there were no examples to enforce
" them.   To attack vices in the abftract, without
" touching perfons, may be fafe fighting indeed, but
" it is fighting with fhadows. My greateft comfort

" and

out of your way to torment declining age,
becaufe the Duke of Bedford may have quarrelled with thofe whofe caufe and politics you
efpoufe? For fhame! for fhame! As you
have *fpoke daggers* to him, you may juftly
dread the *ufe* of them againft your own breaft,
did a want of courage or of noble fentiments ftimulate him to fuch mean revenge.
He is above it; he is brave. Do you fancy
that your own bafe arts have infeded our
whole ifland? But your own reflections,
your own confcience, muft and will, if you
have any fpark of humanity remaining, give
him moft ample vengeance. Not all the
power of words with which you are fo graced,
will ever wafh out, or even palliate this foul
blot in your character. I have not time at
prefent to diffed your letter fo minutely as I
could wifh, but I will be bold enough to fay,
that it is (as to reafon and argument) the
moft extraordinary piece of *florid impotence*
that was ever impofed upon the eyes and ears
of the too credulous and deluded mob. It
accufes the Duke of Bedford of high treafon.
Upon what foundation? You tell us, " that
" the Duke's *pecuniary character* makes it
" more than *probable*, that he could not have
" made fuch facrifices at the peace, without

" and encouragment to proceed has been to fee that
" thofe, who have no fhame, and no fear of any thing
" elfe, have appeared touched by my fatires."

" *fame*

" *some private compensations*; that his conduct
" carried with it an interior evidence, be-
" yond all the legal proofs of a court of
" justice."

My academical education, Sir, bids me
tell you that it is necessary to establish the
truth of your first proposition, before you
presume to draw inferences from it. First
prove the avarice, before you make the rash,
hasty, and most wicked conclusion. This
father, *Junius*, whom you call avaricious,
allowed that son eight thousand pounds a
year. Upon his most unfortunate death,
which your usual good-nature took care to
remind him of, he greatly increased the join-
ture of the afflicted lady, his widow. Is this
avarice? Is this doing good by *stealth*? It is
upon record.

If exact order, method, and true œconomy as a master of a family; if splendor and
just magnificence, without wild waste and
thoughtless extravagance, may constitute the
character of an avaricious man, the Duke is
guilty. But for a moment let us admit that
an ambassador may love money too much;
what proof do you give that he has taken any
to betray his country? Is it hearsay; or the
evidence of letters, or ocular; or the evidence of those concerned in this black affair?
Pro-

Produce your authorities to the public. It is a moſt impudent kind of ſorcery to attempt to blind us with the ſmoke, without convincing us that the fire has exiſted. You firſt brand him, with a vice that he is free from, to render him odious and ſuſpeĉted. Suſpicion is the foul weapon with which you make all your chief attacks; with that you ſtab. But ſhall one of the firſt ſubjeĉts of the realm be ruined in his fame; ſhall even his life be in conſtant danger, from a charge built upon ſuch ſandy foundations? Muſt his houſe be beſieged by lawleſs ruffians, his journies impeded, and even the aſylum of an altar be infecure, from aſſertions ſo baſe and falſe? Potent as he is, the Duke is amenable to juſtice; if guilty, puniſhable. The parliament is the high and ſolemn tribunal for matters of ſuch great moment. To that be they ſubmitted. But I hope alſo that ſome notice will be taken of, and ſome puniſhment inflicted upon falſe accuſers, eſpecially upon ſuch, *Junius*, who are wilfully *falſe*. In any truth I will agree even with *Junius*; will agree with him that it is highly unbecoming the dignity of Peers to tamper with boroughs. Ariſtocracy is as fatal as democracy. Our conſtitution admits of neither. It loves a King, Lords, and Commons really choſen by the unbought ſuffrages of a free people. But if corruption only

ly

ly fhifts hands; if the wealthy commoner
gives the bribe, inftead of the potent Peer, is
the ftate better ferved by this exchange? Is
the real emancipation of the borough effect-
ed, becaufe new parchment bonds may poffibly fuperfede the old? To fay the truth, where-
ever fuch practices prevail, they are equally
criminal to and deftructive of our freedom.

THE reft of your declamation is fcarce
worth confidering, excepting for the elegance of the language. Like Hamlet in the
play, you produce two pictures; you tell us,
that one is not like the Duke of Bedford:
then you bring a moft hideous caricatura,
and tell us of the refemblance; but *multum
cbludit imago.*

ALL your long tedious accounts of the
minifterial quarrels, and the intrigues of the
cabinet, are reducible to a few fhort lines;
and to convince you, Sir, that I do not mean
to flatter any minifter, either paft or prefent,
thefe are my thoughts: they feem to have
acted like lovers, or children; have pouted,
quarrelled, cried, kiffed, and been friends
again, as the objects of defire, the minifterial
rattles *, have been put into their hands. But
.fuch

* SIR WILLIAM's own account of the behaviour of
the Duke and his friends, the men, according to him the
beft

fuch proceedings are very unworthy of the gravity and dignity of a great nation. We do not want men of abilities; but we have wanted fteadinefs; we want unanimity: your letters, *Junius*, will not contribute thereto. You may one day expire by a flame of your own kindling. But it is my humble opinion that lenity and moderation, pardon and oblivion, will difappoint the efforts of all the feditious in the land, and extinguifh their wide fpreading fires. I have lived with this fentiment; with this I fhall die.

WILLIAM DRAPER.

LETTER XL.

TO THE PRINTER OF THE PUBLIC ADVERTISER.

S I R,   13 *October*, 1769.

IF Sir William Draper's bed be a bed of torture, he has made it for himfelf. I fhall never interrupt his repofe. Having changed the fubject, there are parts of his laft letter not undeferving of a reply. Leaving his private character and conduct out of the queftion, I fhall confider him merely in

beft qualified to govern the empire, fhews them in a light perfectly ridiculous.

the

the capacity of an author, whofe labours certainly do no difcredit to a news-paper.

WE fay, in common difcourfe, that a man
may be his own enemy, and the frequency of
the fact makes the expreffion intelligible.   But
that a man fhould be the bittereft enemy of
his friends, implies a contradiction of a pe-
culiar nature.   There is fomething in it,
which cannot be conceived without a confufion of ideas, nor expreffed without a fole-
cifm in language.   Sir William Draper is ftill
that fatal friend Lord Granby found him.
Yet I am ready to do juftice to his generofity; if indeed it be not fomething more than
generous, to be the voluntary advocate of
men, who think themfelves injured by his affiftance, and to confider nothing in the caufe
he adopts, but the difficulty of defending it.
I thought however he had been better read
in the hiftory of the human heart, than to
compare or confound the tortures of the
body with thofe of the mind.   He ought to
have known, though perhaps it might not
be his intereft to confefs, that no outward
tyranny can reach the mind.   If confcience
plays the tyrant, it would be greatly for the
benefit of the world that fhe were more arbitrary, and far lefs placable, than fome men
find her.

BUT.

But it feems I have outraged the feelings of a father's heart.—Am I indeed fo injudicious? Does Sir William Draper think I would have hazarded my credit with a generous nation, by fo grofs a violation of the laws of humanity? Does he think I am fo little acquainted with the firft and nobleft characteriftic of Englifhmen? Or how will he reconcile fuch folly with an underftanding fo full of artifice as mine? Had he been a father, he would have been but little offended with the feverity of the reproach, for his mind would have been filled with the juftice of it. He would have feen that I did not infult the feelings of a father, but the father who felt nothing. He would have trufted to the evidence of his own paternal heart, and boldly denied the poffibility of the fact, inftead of defending it. Againft whom then will his honeft indignation be directed, when I affure him, that this whole town beheld the Duke of Bedford's conduct, upon the death of his fon, with horror and aftonifhment. Sir William Draper does himfelf but little honour in oppofing the general fenfe of his country. The people are feldom wrong in their opinions—in their fentiments they are never miftaken. There may be a vanity perhaps in a fingular way of thinking;—but when a man profeffes a want of thofe feelings, which do honour to the multitude,

he

he hazards fomething infinitely more important than the character of his underftanding.
After all, as Sir William may poffibly be in
earneft in his anxiety for the Duke of Bedford, I fhould be glad to relieve him from it.
He may reft affured this worthy nobleman
laughs, with equal indifference, at my reproaches, and Sir William's diftrefs about
him. But here let it ftop. Even the Duke
of Bedford, infenfible as he is, will confult
the tranquility of his life, in not provoking
the moderation of my temper. If, from the
profoundeft contempt, I fhould ever rife into
anger, he fhould foon find, that all I have already faid of him was lenity and compaffion.

Out of a long catalogue, Sir William
Draper has confined himfelf to the refutation of two charges only. The reft he had
not time to difcufs; and indeed it would
have been a laborious undertaking. To draw
up a defence of fuch a feries of enormities,
would have required a life at leaft as long as
that, which has been uniformly employed in
the practice of them. The public opinion
of the Duke of Bedford's extreme œconomy
is, it feems, entirely without foundation.
Though not very prodigal abroad, in his own
family at leaft he is regular and magnificent.
He pays his debts, abhors a beggar, and
makes a handfome provifion for his fon. His
charity

charity has improved upon the proverb, and ended where it began. Admitting the whole force of this fingle inftance of his domeftic generofity (wonderful indeed, confidering the narrownefs of his fortune, and the little merit of his only fon) the public may ftill perhaps be diffatisfied, and demand fome other lefs equivocal proofs of his munificence. Sir William Draper fhould have entered boldly into the detail—of indigence relieved—of arts encouraged—of fcience patronized; men of learning protected, and works of genius rewarded ;—in fhort, had there been a fingle inftance, befides Mr. Rigby *, of blufhing merit brought forward by the duke, for the fervice of the public, it fhould not have been omitted †.

I WISH it were poffible to eftablifh my inference with the fame certainty, on which I believe the principle is founded. My conclufion however was not drawn from the principle alone. I am not fo unjuft as to reafon from one crime to another ; though I think, that, of all the vices, avarice is moft apt to taint and corrupt the heart. I combined the known temper of the man with

---

* THIS gentleman is fuppofed not to have any idea of *blufhing.*

† THIS paragraph produced the letter from Frances, which follows this.

the extravagant conceffions made by the ambaffador ; and though I doubt not fufficient
care was taken to leave no document of any
treafonable negociation, I ftill maintain that
the conduct * of this minifter carries with it
an internal and convincing evidence againft
him. Sir William Draper feems not to know
the value or force of fuch a proof. He will
not permit us to judge of the motives of men,
by the manifeft tendency of their actions, nor
by the notorious character of their minds. He
calls for papers and witneffes, with a trium-
phant fecurity, as if nothing could be true,
but what could be proved in a court of juftice. Yet a religious man might have remembered, upon what foundation fome
truths, moft interefting to mankind, have
been received and eftablifhed. If it were not
for the internal evidence, which the pureft of
religions carries with it, what would have
become of his once well-quoted decalogue,
and of the meeknefs of his Chriftianity?

THE generous warmth of his refentment
makes him confound the order of events. He
forgets that the infults and diftreffes which
the Duke of Bedford has fuffered, and which

---

* If Sir William Draper will take the trouble of
looking into Torcy's Memoirs, he will fee with what
little ceremony a bribe may be offered to a Duke, and
with what little ceremony it was *only not accepted.*

Sir

Sir William has lamented with many delicate touches of the true pathetic, were only
recorded in my letter to his Grace, not occafioned by it. It was a fimple, candid narrative of facts; though, for aught I know,
it may carry with it fomething prophetic.
His Grace undoubtedly has received feveral
ominous hints; and I think, in certain circumftances, a wife man would do well to
prepare himfelf for the event.

But I have a charge of a heavier nature againft Sir William Draper. He tells
us that the Duke of Bedford is amenable to
juftice;—that parliament is a high and fo-
lemn tribunal; and that, if guilty, he may
be punifhed by due courfe of law; and all
this, he fays, with as much gravity as if he
believed one word of the matter. I hope
indeed, the day of impeachments will arrive,
before this nobleman efcapes out of life;
—but to refer us to that mode of proceeding
now, with fuch a miniftry, and fuch a houfe
of commons as the prefent, what is it, but
an indecent mockery of the common fenfe of
the nation? I think he might have contented himfelf with defending the greateft enemy, without infulting the diftreffes of his
country.

His

HIS concluding declaration of his opinion, with refpect to the prefent condition of affairs, is too loofe and undetermined to be of any fervice to the public. How ftrange is it that this gentleman fhould dedicate fo much time and argument to the defence of worthlefs or indifferent characters, while he gives but feven folitary lines to the only fubject, which can deferve his attention, or do credit to his abilities. ..

JUNIUS.

LETTER XLI.

TO THE PRINTER OF THE PUBLIC ADVERTISER.

SIR, 14 *Oct*, 1769.

PERFECTLY convinced as I am of my own inability to enter the lifts, or ufe my pen, againft the tow-edged fword that glitters in the hand of *Junius*, nothing but my being impelled by that uncommon kind of gratitude, which makes us not only thankful for benefits received, but inclines us to love and refpect our benefactor, could tempt me forth to fo unequal a combat, or prevail on me to offer even a fact to the public, through fuch a channel as our newspapers.

LET

LET my motive then plead my excuse, while I reply to the charge which appears most difficult to be cleared, becaufe it is moſt general, which Junius has made againſt the Duke of Bedford.

JUNIUS calls upon Sir William Draper to " enter boldly into the detail of indigence relieved ; of arts encouraged ; of fcience patronized ; men of learning protected ; and the works of genius rewarded."

UNDER any of thefe denominations, it muſt be extremely painful to a woman, whofe higheſt merit fhould be modeſty, and of courfe a *blufhing merit*, to appear ; yet truth and gratitude ought to furmount female delicacy fo far, as to relate a matter of fact, which fhe hopes will be one proof of the injuſtice of the charge here quoted againſt the Duke of Bedford.

WHEN his Grace was Lord Lieutenant of Ireland, the feries of letters between Henry and Frances happened to fall into his hands. In the preface, Henry fpeaks of the diſtreſſes of his fortune, and the juſtifiable means by which thofe diſtreſſes were occafioned.—His Grace's humanity was affected ; he enquired into the author's fituation, and on finding it to be what is there defcribed, unfolicited by

aught

aught but his own noble nature, he fent for Henry, and, in the moſt obliging and gracious manner, prefented him with a patent employment which was at that time vacant.

SURE I am, that many parallel, perhaps more meritorious, inſtances of his Grace's munificence, might be recounted, if thoſe, who like me, have partaken of them, had virtue fufficient to acknowledge themfelves *obliged*, when they had received an *obligation*.

FRANCES.

LETTER XLII.

TO THE PRINTER OF THE PUBLIC ADVERTISER.

SIR,   20 *October*, 1769.

I VERY fincerely applaud the ſpirit with which a lady has paid the debt of gratitude to her benefactor. Though I think fhe has miftaken the point, fhe fhews a virtue which makes her refpectable. The queſtion turned upon the perſonal generofity or avarice of a man, whoſe private fortune is immenſe. The proofs of his munificence muſt be drawn from the uſes, to which he has applied that fortune. I was not ſpeaking of a Lord Lieute-

.nant

nant of Ireland, but of a rich Englifh duke, whofe wealth gave him the means of doing as much good in this country, as he derived from his power in another. I am far from wifhing to leffen the merit of this fingle benevolent action ;—perhaps it is the more confpicuous from ftanding alone. All I mean to fay is, that it proves nothing in the prefent argument.

JUNIUS.

LETTER XLIII.

SIR,   19 *October*, 1769.

I AM well affured that *Junius* will never defcend to a difpute with fuch a writer as *Modeftus* (whofe letter appeared in the Gazetteer of Monday) efpecially as the difpute muft be chiefly about words. Notwithftanding the partiality of the public, it does not appear that *Junius* values himfelf upon any fuperior fkill in compofition, and I hope his time will always be more ufefully employed than in trifling refinements of verbal criticifm. *Modeftus*, however, fhall have no reafon to triumph in the filence and

L 2   mode-

moderation of *Junius*. If he knew as much
of the propriety of language, as I believe he
does of the facts in queftion, he would have
been as cautious of attacking *Junius* upon his
compofition, as he feems to be of entering
into the fubject of it; yet after all, the laft
is the only article of any importance to the
public.

I Do not wonder at the unremitted rancour
with which the Duke of Bedford and his ad-
herents invariably fpeak of a nation, which
we well know has been too much injured to
be eafily forgiven. But why muft *Junius* be
an Irifhman?—*The abfurdity of his writings
betrays him.*—Waving all confideration of the
infult offered by *Modeftus* to the declared judgment of the people (they may well bear this
among the reft) let us follow the feveral inftances, and try whether the charge be fairly
fupported.

FIRST then,—the leaving a man to enjoy
fuch repofe as he can find upon a bed of torture, is fevere indeed; perhaps too much fo,
when applied to fuch a trifler as Sir William
Draper; but there is nothing abfurd either in
the idea or expreffion. *Modeftus* cannot diftinguifh between a farcafm and a contradiction.

2. I AY-

2. I AFFIRM with *Junius*, that it is the *frequency* of the fact, which alone can make us comprehend how a man can be his own enemy. We should never arrive at the complex idea conveyed by these words, if we had only seen one or two instances of a man acting to his own prejudice. Offer the proposition to a child, or a man unused to compound his ideas, and you will soon see how little either of them understand you. It is not a simple idea arising from a single fact, but a very complex idea arising from many facts well observed, and accurately compared.

3. MODESTUS could not, without great affectation, mistake the meaning of *Junius*, when he speaks of a man who is the bitterest enemy of his friends. He could not but know, that *Junius* spoke, not of a false or hollow friendship, but of a real intention to serve, and that intention producing the worst effects of enmity. Whether the description be strictly applicable to Sir William Draper is another question. *Junius* does not say that it is more *criminal* for a man to be the enemy of his friends than his own, though he might have affirmed it with truth. In a moral light a man may certainly take greater liberties with himself than with another. To sacrifice ourselves merely is a weakness we may indulge in, if we think proper, for we do it at our own

L 3 hazard

hazard and expence ; but, under the pretence
of friendſhip, ts ſport with the reputation, or
ſacrifice the honour of another, is ſomething
worſe than weakneſs ; and if, in favour of
the fooliſh intention, we do not call it a crime,
we muſt allow at leaſt that it ariſes from an
overweening, buſy, meddling impudence.——
Junius ſays only, and he ſays truly, that it is
more extraordinary, that it involves a greater
contradiction than the other ; and is it not a
maxim received in life, that in general we can
determine more wiſely for others than for
ourſelves ? The reaſon of it is ſo clear in
argument, that it hardly wants the confirmation of experience. Sir William Draper, I
confeſs, is an exception to the general rule,
though not much to his credit.

4. IF this gentleman will go back to his
Ethicks, he may perhaps diſcover the truth of
what *Junius* ſays, *that no outward tyranny can
reach the mind.* The tortures of the body
may be introduced by way of ornament or
illuſtration to repreſent thoſe of the mind, but
ſtrictly there is no ſimilitude between them.
They are totally different both in their cauſe
and operation. The wretch, who ſuffers upon
the rack, is merely paſſive ; but when the
mind is tortured, it is not at the command of
any outward power. It is the ſenſe of guilt
which conſtitutes the puniſhment, and creates
that

that torture with which the guilty mind acts
upon itself.

5. He misquotes what *Junius* says of confcience, and makes the fentence ridiculous,
by making it his own.

So much for compofition. Now for fact.—
Junius it feems has miftaken the duke of Bedford. His Grace had all the proper feelings of
a father, though he took care to fupprefs the
appearance of them. Yet it was an occafion,
one would think, on which he need not have
been afhamed of his grief ;—on which lefs
fortitude would have done him more honour.
I can conceive indeed a benevolent motive for
his endeavouring to affume an air of tranquil-
lity in his own family, and I wifh I could
difcover any thing, in the reft of his character,
to juftify my affigning that motive to his behaviour. But is there no medium ? Was it
neceffary to appear abroad, to ballot at the
India-houfe, and make a public difplay, tho'
it were only of an apparent infenfibility?—I
know we are treading on tender ground, and
Junius, I am convinced, does not wifh to urge
this queftion farther. Let the friends of the
Duke of Bedford obferve that humble filence, which becomes their fituation. They
fhould recollect that there are ftill fome

facts * in ftore, at which human nature would
fhudder. I fhall be underftood by thofe whom
it concerns, when I fay that thefe facts go farther † than to the Duke.

It is not incohfiftent to fuppofe that a man
may be quite indifferent about one part of a
charge, yet feverely ftung with another, and
though he feels no remorfe, that he may wifh
to be revenged. The charge of infenfibility
carries a reproach indeed, but no danger with
it.—*Junius* had faid, *there are others who
would affaffinate.* *Modeftus,* knowing his
man, will not fuffer the infinuation to be
divided, but fixes it all upon the Duke of
Bedford.

Without determining upon what evi-
dence *Junius* would *choofe to be condemned*, I will
venture to maintain, in oppofition to *Modeftus,* or to Mr. Rigby (who is certainly not

* The Duke had an inventory taken of the Marquis's clothes, fold them all, and pocketed the money:
but the Marchionefs gave her late husband's fervant the
value of them out of her own pocket.

† When the incomparable Marchionefs died, the
Duchefs of Bedford, her mother in law, had all her
wearing apparel fold, and put the money in her pocket.
In a fortnight after the unfortunate death of the Mar-
quis, his mother the Duchefs had a route at Bedford
Houfe.

Modeftus)

Modeſtus) or any other of the Bloomſbury gang, that the evidence againſt the Duke of Bedford is as ſtrong as any preſumptive evidence can be. It depends upon a combination of facts and reaſoning, which require no confirmation from the anecdote of the Duke of Marlborough. This anecdote was referred to merely to ſhew how ready a great man may be to receive a great bribe ; and if *Modeſtus* could read the original, he would ſee that the expreſſion, *only not accepted*, was probably the only one in our language that exactly fitted the caſe. The bribe, offered to the Duke of Marlborough, was not refuſed.

I CANNOT conclude without taking notice of this honeſt gentleman's learning, and wiſhing he had given us a little more of it. When he accidentally found himſelf ſo near ſpeaking truth, it was rather unfair of him to leave out the *non potuiſſe refelli.* As it ſtands, the *pudet hæc opprobria* may be divided equally between Mr. Rigby and the Duke of Bedford. Mr. Rigby, I take for granted, will aſſert his natural right to the modeſty of the quotation, and leave all the opprobrium to his Grace.

PHILO JUNIUS.

L 5   LETTER

LETTER XLIV.

TO THE PRINTER OF THE PUBLIC ADVERTISER.

SIR,   27 *October*, 1769..

IT is not wonderful that the great cause, in which this country is engaged, should have roused and engrossed the whole attention of the people. I rather admire the generous spirit, with which they feel and assert their interest in this important question, than blame them for their indifference about any other. When the constitution is openly invaded, when the first original right of the people, from which all laws derive their authority, is directly attacked, inferior grievances naturally lose their force, and are suffered to pass by without punishment or observation. The present ministry are as singularly marked by their fortune, as by their crimes. Instead of atoning for their former conduct by any wise or popular measure, they have found, in the enormity of one fact, a cover and defence for a series of measures, which must have been fatal to any other administration. I fear we are too remiss in observing the whole of their proceedings.

ings. Struck with the principal figure, we
do not fufficiently mark in what manner.
the canvafs is filled up. Yet furely it is not
a lefs crime, nor lefs fatal in its confequences, to encourage a flagrant breach of the·
law by a military force, than to make ufe of
the forms of parliament to deftroy the confti--
tution.—The miniftry feem determined to
give us a choice of difficulties, and, if pofli--
ble, ' to perplex us with the multitude of
their offences. The expedient is worthy of
the Duke of Grafton. But though he has
preferved a gradation and variety in his meafures, we fhould remember that the principle
is uniform. Dictated by the fame fpirit,
they deferve the fame attention. The follow--
ing fact, though of the moft alarming nature,
has not yet been clearly ftated to the public,
nor have the confequences of it been fufficiently underftood. Had I taken it up at an
earlier period, I fhould have been accufed of
an uncandid, malignant precipitation, as if·
I watched for an unfair advantage againft'
the miniftry, and would not allow them a·
reafonable time to do their duty. They now
ftand without excufe. Inftead of employing:
the leifure they have had, in a ftrict exami-
nation of the offence, and punifhing the offenders, they feem to have confidered *that*
indulgence as a fecurity to them, that, with
a little time and management, the whole af-

L 6 fair

fair might be buried in silence, and utterly
forgotten.

A Major General of the army * is arrested
by the sheriff's officers for a considerable debt.
                                              He

* Major General William Gansell, of the
55th regiment. He was a great connoisseur, particularly in paintings, of which he had a very large and valuable collection ; he also possessed a very considerable
estate, besides the emoluments he derived from his profession ; but his passion for paintings greatly embar-
rassed his circumstances. He was nephew to the celebrated Dr. Ward, who at his death, December 1761,
left him all the money he owed him by bond or other-
wise, any three of his pictures the General should
choose, and one thousand pounds in money.

Saturday, May 21st, 1770, the following order
came out to the brigade of guards. Parole Hounslow.

B. O. His Majesty has signified to the field officer
in waiting, that he has been acquainted that Serjeant
Bacon of the first regiment, and Serjeant Parke of the
Coldstream regiment ; William Powell, William Hart,
James Potter, and Joseph Collins, private soldiers in
the first regiment of foot guards, were more or less concerned in the rescue of Major General Gansell, in September last ; the King hopes, and is willing to believe,
they did not know the Major General was arrested, and
only thought they were delivering an officer in distress ;
however his Majesty commands, that they should be
severely reprimanded for acting in this business as they
have done ; and strictly orders for the future, that no
non commissioned officer or soldier do presume to in-
                                              terfere

He perfuades them to conduct him to the Tilt-yard in St. James's Park, under fome pretence of bufinefs, which it imported him to fettle before he was confined. He applies to a ferjeant, not immediately on duty, to affift

fere with bailiffs, or arrefts, on any account or pre-tence whatfoever, the crime being of a very atrocious nature ; and if any are found guilty of difobeying this order, they will be moft feverely punifhed. This order to be read immediately at the head of every company in the brigade of guards, that no man may plead igno-rance for the future.

THE General ftill continuing involved in debt, five bailiffs, two Hydes, Felthoufe, Sly, and Reeves, at the fuit of Samuel Lee, a furgeon, went on the 26th of Auguft 1773, to arreft him at his apartments in Craven Street, for the fum of of 134l. The General made re-fiftance on being attacked in his own apartments, by firing two piftols through the door, but the bailiffs broke in upon him, and carried him off. On the 14th of Sep-tember, the General was tried at the Old Bailey for his life for firing the piftols. The bailiffs fwore what they thought neceffary to convict him. But Mr. Juftice Nares obferved, that confidering the evidence of the two Hydes and Felthoufe by itfelf, without at all looking to what the evidences for the General had fworn, it was al-together improbable and contradictory, and pointed out parts of it which could not poffibly be believed. The Jury were of the Judge's opinion, and immediately brought in a verdict of Not Guilty, without going out of Court. The General in his defence mentioned that he had read in Blackftone's Commentaries, that an Eng-lifhman's

affift with fome of his companions in favour-
ing his efcape.   He attempts it.   A buftle
enfues.   The bailiffs claim their prifoner.
† An officer of the guards, not then on duty,
takes part in the affair, applies to the ‡ lieutenant commanding the Tilt-yard guard,
and urges him to turn out his guard to relieve a general officer.   The lieutenant de-
clines interfering in perfon, but ftands at a
diftance, and fuffers the bufinefs to be done.
The officer takes upon himfelf to order out
the guard.   In a moment they are in arms,
quit their guard, march, refcue the general,
and drive away the fheriffs officers, who, in
vain reprefent their right to the prifoner, and
the nature of the arreft.   The foldiers firft
conduct the general into the guard-room,
then efcort him to a place of fafety, with bay-
onets fixed, and in all the forms of military

lifhman's houfe was his caftle, and that he had lived in
the apartments in which he was attacked thirty-eight
years.   He was however detained upon the arreft, and
committed to the Fleet Prifon, where he died fuddenly
on the 28th of July 1774.   He was a very ftout man,
but corpulent; his death was imputed to the burfting
of a blood veffel.

† LIEUTENANT DODD.

‡ LIEUTENANT GARTH, now a Brigadier General in the Weft Indies, and an excellent officer.

triumph.

triumph. I will not enlarge upon the various circumſtances which attended this a-.
trocious proceeding. The perſonal injury
received by the officers of the law in the execution of their duty, may perhaps be atoned
for by ſome private compenſation. I. conſider nothing but the wound, which has been.
given to the law itſelf, to which no reme-.
dy has been applied, no ſatisfaction made.
Neither is it my deſign to dwell upon the
miſconduct of the parties concerned, any farther than is neceſſary to ſhew the behaviour.
of the miniſtry in its true light. I would
make every compaſſionate allowance for the
infatuation of the priſoner, the falſe and criminal diſcretion of one officer, and the madneſs of another. I would leave the ignorant
ſoldiers entirely out of the queſtion. They
are certainly the leaſt guilty, though they are
the only perſons who have yet ſuffered, even
in the appearance of puniſhment †. The
fact itſelf, however atrocious, is not the
principal point to be conſidered. It might
have happened under a more regular government, and with guards better diſciplined
than ours. The main queſtion is, in what
manner have the miniſtry acted on this extraordinary occaſion. A general officer calls
upon the king's own guard, then actually on

† Some of them were confined.

duty, to refcue him from the laws of his country; yet in this moment he is in a fituation
no worfe, than if he had not committed an
offence, equally enormous in a civil and military view.—A lieutenant upon duty defignedly quits his guard, and fuffers it to be
drawn out by another officer, for a purpofe,
which he well knew (as we may collect
from an appearance of caution, which only
makes his behaviour the more criminal) to
be in the higheft degree illegal. Has this
gentleman been called to a court martial to
anfwer for his conduct? No. Has it been
cenfured? No. Has it been in any fhape enquired into? No.—Another lieutenant, not
upon duty, nor even in his regimentals, is
daring enough to order out the king's guard,
over which he had properly no command,
and engages them in a violation of the laws
of his country, perhaps the moft fingular
and extravagant that ever was attempted—
What punifhment has *he* fuffered? Literally
none. Suppofing he fhould be profecuted
at common law for the refcue, will that circumftance, from which the miniftry can derive no merit, excufe or juftify their fuffer-
ing fo flagrant a breach of military difcipline
to pafs by unpunifhed, and unnoticed?
Are they aware of the outrage offered to their
fovereign, when his own proper guard is ordered out to ftop by main force the execu-

tion

tion of his laws? What are we to conclude from fo fcandalous a neglect of their duty, but that they have other views, which can only be anfwered by fecuring the attachment of the guards? The minifter would hardly be fo cautious of offending them, if he did not mean, in due time, to call for their affiftance.

With refpect to the parties themfelves, let it be obferved, that thefe gentlemen are neither young officers, nor very young men. Had they belonged to the unfledged race of enfigns, who infeft our ftreets, and difhonour our public places, it might perhaps be fufficient to fend them back to that difcipline, from which their parents, judging lightly from the maturity of their vices, had removed them too foon. In this cafe, I am forry to fee, not fo much the folly of youth, as the fpirit of the corps, and the connivance of government. I do not queftion that there are many brave and worthy officers in the regiments of guards. But confidering them as a corps, I fear, it will be found that they are neither good foldiers, nor good fubjects. Far be it from me to infinuate the moft diftant reflection upon the army. On the contrary, I honour and efteem the profeffion; and if thefe gentlemen were better foldiers, I am fure they would be better fubjects. It

is

is not that there is any internal vice or defect in the profession itself, as regulated in
this country, but that it is the spirit of this
particular corps, to despise their profession,
and that while they vainly assume the lead of
the army, they make it matter of impertinent
comparison, and triumph over the bravest
troops in the world (I mean our marching
regiments) that *they* indeed stand, upon
higher ground, and are privileged to neglect the laborious forms of military discipline
and duty. Without dwelling longer upon
a most invidious subject, I shall leave it to
military men, who have seen a service more
active than the parade, to determine whether
or no I speak truth.

How far this dangerous spirit has been encouraged by government, and to what pernicious purposes it may be applied hereafter,
well deserves our most serious consideration.
I know indeed, that when this affair happened,
an affectation of alarm ran through the ministry. Something must be done to save appearances. The case was too flagrant to be
passed by absolutely without notice. But how
have they acted? Instead of ordering the officers concerned, (and who, strictly speaking,
are alone guilty) to be put under arrest, and
brought to trial, they would have it understood, that they did their duty completely, in
con-

confining a ferjeant and four private foldiers, until they fhould be demanded by the civil power; fo that while the officers, who ordered or permitted the thing to be done, efcape without cenfure, the poor men who, obeyed, thofe orders, who in a military view are no way refponfible for what they did, and who for that reafon have been difcharged by the civil magiftrates, are the only objects whom the miniftry have thought proper to expofe to punifhment. They did not venture to bring even thefe men to a court martial, becaufe they knew their evidence would be fatal to fome perfons, whom they were determined to protect. Otherwife, I doubt not, the lives of thefe unhappy, friendlefs foldiers, would long fince have been facrificed without fcruple, to the fecurity of their guilty officers.

I HAVE been accufed of endeavouring to, enflame the paffions of the people.—Let me, now appeal to their underftanding. If there be any tool of adminiftration daring enough, to deny thefe facts, or fhamelefs enough to defend the conduct of the miniftry, let him come forward. I care not under what title he appears. He fhall find me ready to maintain the truth of my narrative, and the juftice of my obfervations upon it, at the hazard of my utmoft credit with the public.

UNDER

UNDER the moſt arbitrary governments, the common adminiſtration of juſtice is ſuffered to take its courſe. The ſubject, though robbed of his ſhare in the legiſlature, is ſtill protected by the laws. The political freedom of the Engliſh conſtitution was once the pride and honour of an Engliſhman. The civil equality of the laws preſerved the property, and defended the ſafety of the ſubject. Are theſe glorious privileges the birthright of the people, or are we only tenants at the will of the miniſtry?—But that I know there is a ſpirit of reſiſtance in the hearts of my countrymen, that they value life, not by its conveniencies, but by the independence and dignity of their condition, I ſhould, at this moment, appeal only to their diſcretion. I ſhould perſuade them to baniſh from their minds all memory of what we were; I ſhould tell them this is not a time to remember that we were Engliſhmen; and give it as my laſt advice, to make ſome early agreement with the miniſter, that ſince it has pleaſed him to rob us of thoſe political rights, which once diſtinguiſhed the inhabitants of a country, where honour was happineſs, he would leave us at leaſt the humble, obedient ſecurity of citizens, and graciouſly condeſcend to protect us in our ſubmiſſion.

JUNIUS.

LETTER

L E T T E R XLV.

TO THE PRINTER OF THE PUBLIC AD-
VERTISER.

S I R,   *November* 14, 1769.

THE variety of remarks which have
been made upon the laſt letter of
Junius, and my own opinion of the writer,
who, whatever may be his faults, is certainly not a weak man, have induced me to
examine, with ſome attention, the ſubject
of that letter. I could not perſuade myſelf
that, while he had plenty of important materials, he would have taken up a light or trifling occaſion to attack the miniſtry; much
leſs could I conceive that it was his intention to ruin the officers concerned in the reſ-
cue of General Ganſell, or to injure the General himſelf. Theſe are little objects, and
can no way contribute to the great purpoſes
he ſeems to have in view by addreſſing himſelf to the public.——Without conſidering
the ornamented ſtile he has adopted, I determined to look farther into the matter, before
I decided upon the merits of his letter. The
firſt ſtep I took was to enquire into the truth
of the facts; for if theſe were either falſe or
miſre-

misreprefented, the moft artful exertion of his underftanding, in reafoning upon them, would only be a difgrace to him.—Now, Sir, I have found every circumftance ftated by *Junius* to be literally true. General Ganfell perfuaded the bailiffs to conduct him to the parade, and certainly folicited a corporal and other foldiers to affift him in making his efcape. Captain Dodd * did certainly apply to Captain Garth for the affiftance of his guard. Captain Garth declined appearing himfelf, but ftood aloof, while the other took upon him to order out the King's guard, and by main force refcued the General. It is alfo ftrictly true, that the General was efcorted by a file of mufqueteers to a place of fecurity. —Thefe are facts, Mr. Woodfall, which I promife you no gentleman in the guards will deny. If all or any of them are falfe, why are they not contradicted by the parties them-felves? However fecure againft military cen-fure, they have yet a character to lofe, and furely, if they are innocent, it is not beneath them to pay fome attention to the opinion of the public.

THE force of *Junius's* Obfervations upon thefe facts cannot be better marked, than by

---

* Dodd and Garth, though only lieutenants, had captains rank. All the lieutenants of the Guards have captains rank.

ftating

ftating and refuting the objections which
have been made to them. One writer fays,
" Admitting the officers have offended, they
" are punifhable at common law, and will
" you have a Britifh fubject punifhed twice
" for the fame offence ?"—I anfwer that
they have committed two offences, both very
enormous, and violated two laws. The
refcue is one offence, the flagrant breach of
difcipline another, and hitherto it does not
appear that they have been punifhed, or even
cenfured for either. Another gentleman
lays much ftrefs upon the calamity of the cafe,
and inftead of difproving facts, appeals at
once to the compaffion of the public. This
idea, as well as the infinuation, that *depriving
the parties of their commiffions would be an injury
to their creditors*, can only refer to General
Ganfell. The other officers are in no diftrefs, therefore have no claim to compaffion,
nor does it appear, that their creditors, if they
have any, are more likely to be fatisfied by
their continuing in the guards. But this
fort of plea will not hold in any fhape.
Compaffion to an offender, who has grofsly
violated the laws, is in effect a cruelty to the
peaceable fubject who has obferved them ;
and, even admitting the force of any alleviat-
ing circumftances, it is neverthelefs true,
that, in this inftance, the royal compaffion
has interpofed too foon. The legal and proper

per mercy of a King of England may remit
the punishment, but ought not to stop the
trial.

BESIDES these particular objections, there
has been a cry raised against *Junius* for his
malice and injustice in attacking the ministry upon an event, which they could neither
hinder nor foresee.   This, I must affirm, is
a false representation of his argument.   He
lays no stress upon the event itself, as a
ground of accusation against the ministry,
but dwells entirely upon their subsequent
conduct.   He does not say that they are an-
swerable for the offence, but for the scandalous neglect of their duty, in suffering an offence, so flagrant, to pass by without notice
or inquiry.   Supposing them ever so regard-
less of what they owe to the public, and as
indifferent about the opinion as they are
about the interests of their country, what answer, as officers of the crown, will they give
to *Junius,* when he asks them, *Are they aware
of the outrage offered to their Sovereign, when
his own proper guard is ordered out to stop, by
main force, the execution of his laws ?*—And
when we see a ministry giving such a strange
unaccountable protection to the officers of
the guards, is it unfair to suspect, that they
have some secret and unwarrantable motives
for their conduct ?   If they feel themselves injured

jured by fuch a fufpicion, why do they not immediately clear themfelves from it, by doing their duty? For the honour of the guards, I cannot help expreffing another fufpicion, that if the commanding officer had not received a 'fecret injunction to the contrary, he would, in the ordinary courfe of his bufinefs, have applied for a ccurt martial to try the two fubalterns; the one for quitting his guard—the other for taking upon him the command of the guard, and employing it in the manner he did. I do not mean to enter into or defend the feverity, with which *Junius* treats the guards. On the contrary, I will fuppofe for a moment, that they deferve a very different character. If this be true, in what light will they confider the conduct of the two fubalterns, but as a general reproach and difgrace to the whole corps? And will they not wifh to fee them cenfured in a military way, if it were only for the credit and difcipline of the regiment.

Upon the whole, Sir, the Miniftry feem to me to have taken a very improper advantage of the good-nature of the public, whofe humanity, they found, confidered nothing in this affair but the diftrefs of General Ganfell. They would perfuade us that it was only a common refcue by a few diforderly foldiers, and not the formal deliberate act of the king's guard, headed by an officer, and the public has fallen into the deception. I think, therefore, we are obliged to *Junius* for the care he has taken to enquire into the facts, and for the juft commentary with which he has given them to the world.—For my own part, I am as unwilling as any man to load the unfortunate; but, really, Sir, the precedent, with refpect to the guards, is of a moft important nature, and alarming enough (confidering the confequences with which it may be attended) to deferve a parliamentary enquiry: when the guards are daring enough, not only to violate their own difcipline, but publicly and with the moft atrocious violence to ftop the execution of the laws, and when fuch extraordinary offences pafs with impunity, believe me, Sir, the precedent ftrikes deep.

PHILO JUNIUS.

LETTER

L E T T E R XLVI.

T O J U N I U S.

S I R,

YOU challenge any tool of adminiftration to defend the conduct of miniftry.
I accept of your challenge, though it is not
addreffed to me. I am no tool of adminiftration, but your equal, Junius, perhaps
your fuperior in every thing that may become
a man. I defire, for judges of the conteft,
juftice, candour, and impartiality—I dare
you to your uttermoft, and if I do not make
you appear in the eyes of all reafonable men,
as contemptible as you deferve to be, let the
fcorn be transferred to myfelf.

You fay you will defend the truth of your
narrative, and the juftice of your obfervations, at the rifk of your " *utmoft credit.*"
The rifk is fmall, but it is all you have, and
therefore I take you at your word. Facts
that come from Junius are liable to fufpicion; but here he is fupported by public
fame. All the facts in your tedious narrative
I have heard before; and the only new in-
M 2   forma-

formation you have given the public is, that one of the officers engaged in this affair was not in regimentals. But though I have heard all, and am probably inclined to believe that the greateft part is true, I would not be underftood to vouch for any. On the other hand, I will not imitate you, and affert when I cannot prove; let the fact therefore be thrown out of difpute, till it is better afcertained, and let the juftice of your obfervations be my prefent fubject.

You accufe the minifter of a crime, in relation to the arreft of a general officer: I afk you what that crime is? Had he fcreened and protected an officer of the higheft rank from juftice, I could have underftood you, and the cafe would have been truly alarming; but were you to fay fo, the falfehood would be confuted by the perfonal knowledge of all men. Tender of the regular execution of juftice, the minifter interpofed beyond his province in fupport of it; I fay, beyond his province; and had your judgment been equal to your malice, you would have accufed him of interfering in the execution of the law, without being required by the civil power. You do not fee where you attempt to lead a deluded people. If you had known the conftitution, if you ferioufly meant it well, you never would have made it a crime in the minifter

nifter that he did not do more; you might, with fome appearance, have blamed him for interpofing at all.

YET even then, his crime would have been a zeal, perhaps an officious zeal, to fecure criminals, who, by their low rank and fitua-tion, might be naturally fufpected of a defign to withdraw themfelves from juftice. But you fay this was only to fave appearances; and your proof is, that the officers were not. fecured. The officers were not fecured, be-caufe there was no fear of their. running a-way. They are ftill open to a profecution; and if the fpirit of the times is fuch, that no indulgence can be given for an offence fo common, and generally confidered as a venial one, let the utmoft feverity of the law be ex-erted againft them; and I could wifh it were exerted againft many other greater offenders.

IT would, perhaps, be unjuft to accufe you of enforcing the enormity of the crime from enmity to the criminals. I am certain it would be ridiculous to fuppofe you enforced it from refpect to the laws. But a minifter was to be wounded; and provided this could be done, no matter through whofe fide the weapon ftruck. I do not dwell on the bar-barity of attempting to load the unfortunate. You tell a generous nation, that the principal

perfon concerned is in no worfe fituation than
if he had not committed the offence; but
you take care to lead its attention from what
his fituation is.   You dare not venture to
expofe to the compaffion of a generous nation, a man of fome rank, ruined, and in
prifon; and you prefent no objects but fuch
as are calculated to inflame; when humanity
fhould have prompted you to prefent the moft
proper to extenuate.

We know what the common law decrees
in offences of this nature; and it requires not
the help of Junius to execute its decrees. But
he fays the offenders fhould be punifhed alfo
by military law.   Perhaps, in rigour, they
fhould: but are we only to liften to the voice
of feverity? And is Junius the man who
bids us fhut our ears to indulgence? Where
was his zeal for the law when the peace of
this capital was difturbed by a lawlefs mob?
And why did not Junius arraign the conduct
of a minifter, whofe lenity overlooked the
moft grofs infult that ever was offered to order? When the king was, in a manner, befieged in his palace, a compaffionate refpect
for the delufion of a multitude withheld that
exertion of power which the law authorifed.
Did Junius then ftand forth the champion
of his outraged fovereign? No, he dignified
the infult with an honourable name, and
branded

branded the moderation of government with
a name of infamy. But let two inconfidera-
ble officers, from inconfiderate regard to one
of fuperior rank, affift him to efcape from
a bailiff, and Junius is immediately in arms.
The conftitution is already ruined, and private property is no longer fecure. What if
the king only delays that military punifhment, which you are fo anxious to have inflicted, only to fecure the creditors payment?
If thefe people are broke, the debt is loft.
But were the king and his minifters to act
with the purity and the wifdom of angels,
your heart would find fomething amifs, and
your paultry intereft of a day would compel
you to utter your cenfure.

BLINDNESS herfelf muft fee through the
purpofe of the invidious comparifon you draw
between the guards and the marching regiments. *Divide et impera*, is a maxim you
underftand: but happily for this nation, you
are but a bungler in the application of it.
The guards defpife your malicious invectives,
as the reft of the army do your infidious enco-
miums. You fay, the minifter is tender of
the guards, becaufe, in due time, he will make
ufe of them. I hope, if the conftitution is
attacked, not only they, but every good fubject in the kingdom will ftand up in its defence. But you will not fucceed in your de-

M 4   fign

fign to make your party begin that attack, by
perfuading them that force may be firft employed againft themfelves. The experienced
lenity of government is proof againft your
fedition, and though your defperation would
involve *all* in ruin, you will not find a *part*
difpofed to fupport you.

To conclude: your letter is a dull invective.
The ftory you tell has neither the charm of
novelty, or fpirit to recommend it. The
confequences you draw from an incident,
which you admit to be a very common one,
are as abfurd as they are malicious. And in
your preface and peroration, you refemble
thofe termagent women, who, whilft they
are tearing out the eyes of a hufband who
does not defend himfelf, never ceafe the cry
of murder.   MODESTUS.

                              LETTER

LETTER XLVII.

TO JUNIUS.

SIR,

THREE weeks are elapsed since you favoured the public with an essay on the arrest of a general officer. You wrested the circumstances with which it was attended, into a crime against administration. You told the story in your own way; you reasoned upon it in your own way also; you abused, you praised, you challenged, and you concluded. In all this, it would be difficult to decide, whether the inveteracy of your malice, the absurdity of your argument, the barbarity of your intention, or the dulness of your stile and composition, appeared most conspicuous.

But, Sir, waving the rest, you challenged, and these are the precise terms of your defiance : ' I have been accused of endeavouring ' to inflame the passions of the people, &c.'

Two days after your letter made its appearance in the Public Advertiser, an answer to it appeared in the Gazetteer, in which

your challenge was accepted in the following words : ' You challenge any tool of admi-
' niſtration to defend the conduct of the mi-
' niſtry ; I accept of your challenge, though
' it is not addreſſed to me.　I am no tool of
' adminiſtration, but your equal, Junius,
' perhaps your ſuperior, in every thing that
' may become a man.　I deſire for judges
' of the conteſt, juſtice, candour, and impar-
' tiality.　I dare you to the uttermoſt ; and
' if I do not make you appear, in the eyes of
' all reaſonable men, as contemptible as you
' deſerve to be, let the ſcorn be transferred
' to myſelf.'

WHAT is the reaſon, Junius, that you
have hitherto taken no notice of that letter ?
The author of it, too candid to affirm what
he could not immediately prove, ſuppoſed, in
his argument, your narrative to be true ; and
even on that ſuppoſition, he demonſtrated
your obſervations not only unjuſt, but in-
conſiſtent, even to abſurdity.　But if he could
not with certain knowledge deny the fact,
he doubted it ; he told you ſo ; and in the
belief that no man would give a formal chal-
lange without purſuing it, he has enquired
into the truth of that fact.　He tells you now,
and will maintain it at the utmoſt hazard of
his credit with the public, that your narrative
is no leſs falſe than your obſervations are fallacious.

lacious. It is falfe (for inftance) that the general officer applied to a ferjeant, not on duty, to favour his efcape. It is falfe, that the officer of the guard ftood at a, diftance, and fuffered the bufinefs to be done. He was fpoken to by the other officer in the coffee-houfe, and he not only declined interfering in perfon, but flatly refufed his affiftance directly or indirectly. He did more : he dif-fuaded his brother officer from his intention, and believed he had prevailed. His only fault was, being the dupe of the other's ap-parent repentance, who left the coffee-houfe, as if he intended to proceed no farther in the attempt; and took the opportunity to apply to fome foldiers of the guard, while the offi-cer who commanded it remained at the cof-fee-houfe. It is falfe that the guard was turned out, or under arms. And it is a moft malicious conftruction of the faireft conduct, to blame adminiftration, becaufe thefe gentlemen have not been punifhed by mili-tary law.

THE truth is, that it was propofed to try the offenders by military law, immediately after the offence was committed; but, in a confultation with the civil magiftrate, it was judged improper, left a military trial fhould prejudge the action now depending, and in which the offenders are at prefent under bail.

A fair

A fair trial is the right of every Englishman, whatever offence he may be guilty of. Our civil rights are our moſt precious bleſſings; and our form of trial is the bulwark of theſe rights; and, Sir, you contradict the principles you profeſs, when you endeavour to ſet up martial, in oppoſition to common law, and give that the lead which ought to follow. Had theſe gentlemen been firſt tried by military law, the evidences brought before a court martial muſt have been afterwards examined in the courts of law; but witneſſes already examined upon oath, according to the arbitrary proceedings of a court martial, cannot be unexceptionable in a ſubſequent civil action. Their evidence, however extorted, would awe them to conceal, or diſguiſe the truth, which our form of civil trial is ſo well calculated to diſcover. And you, Junius, a patriot, and an aſſertor of the rights of Engliſhmen, would have declaimed and exclaimed, with ſome appearance of juſtice, againſt the proceedings of a court martial, which ſhould have deprived theſe officers of that fair and legal trial which they have a right, as Engliſhmen, to demand.

Our military laws preſcribe the puniſhment of caſhiering for offences of this nature. But how is this crime to be proved? Only by the verdict of a jury in a civil action;

tion; and the judgment upon it is evidence
of record in the fubfequent court martial:
but thefe are matters of which you are ignorant. You go on in your old method, to
clap the cart before the horfe; and you
would have punifhed by military law, an
offence which military law cannot take cog-
nizance of, until it has been legally found
one by the verdict of a jury. Thus, blind-
ed by your paffion, or unacquainted with the
conftitution, you would overturn it, to
wreck your refentment againft a miniftry,
which, in this inftance at leaft, has acted in
its trueft fpirit.

IT is time, Junius, you fhould think of
the challenge you gave. I know you to be
flow, and I have not hurried you.

MODESTUS.

LETTER

LETTER XLVIII.

TO THE PRINTER OF THE PUBLIC ADVERTISER.

SIR,   15 *Nov.* 1769.

I ADMIT the claim of a gentleman, who publishes in the Gazetteer under the name of *Modestus*. He has some right to expect an answer from me; though, I think, not so much from the merit or importance of his objections, as from my own voluntary engagement. I had a reason for not taking notice of him sooner, which, as he is a candid person, I believe he will think sufficient. In my first letter, I took for granted, from the time which had elapsed, that there was no intention to censure, nor even to try the persons concerned in the rescue of General Gansell; but *Modestus* having since either affirmed, or strongly insinuated, that the offenders might still be brought to a legal trial, any attempt to prejudge the cause, or to prejudice the minds of a jury, or a court martial, would be highly improper.

A MAN, more hostile to the ministry than I am, would not so often remind them of
their

their duty. If the Duke of Grafton will not perform the duty of his ftation, why is he minifter?—I will not defcend to a fcurrilous altercation with any man : but this is a fubject too important to be pafled over with filent indifference. If the gentlemen, whofe conduct is in queftion, are not brought to a trial, the Duke of Grafton fhall hear from me again. -

THE motives on which I am fuppofed to have taken up this caufe, are of little importance, compared with the facts themfelves, and the obfervations I have made upon them. Without a vain profeffion of integrity, which, in thefe times might juftly be fufpected, I fhall fhew myfelf in effect a friend to the interefts of my countrymen, and leave it to them to determine, whether I am moved by a perfonal malevolence to three private gentlemen, or merely by a hope of perplexing the miniftry, or whether I am animated by a juft and honourable purpofe of obtaining a fatisfaction to the laws of this country, equal, if poffible, to the violation they have fuffered.

JUNIUS.

LETTER

LETTER XLIX.

TO HIS GRACE THE DUKE OF GRAFTON.

MY LORD,   29 *Nov.* 1769.

THOUGH my opinion of your Grace's integrity was but little affected by the coyness with which you received Mr. Vaughan's proposals, I confess I give you some credit for your discretion. You had a fair opportunity of displaying a certain delicacy, of which you had not been suspected; and you were in the right to make use of it. By laying in a moderate stock of reputation, you undoubtedly meant to provide for the future necessities of your character, that with an honourable resistance upon record, you might safely indulge your genius, and yield to a favourite inclination with security. But you have discovered your purposes too soon; and, instead of the modest reserve of virtue, have shewn us the termagent chastity of a prude, who gratifies her passions with distinction, and prosecutes one lover for a rape, while she solicits the lewd embraces of another.

YOUR:

YOUR cheek turns pale ; for a guilty con-
science tells you, you are undone.—Come
forward, thou virtuous minifter, and tell the
world by what intereft Mr. Hine has been
recommended to fo extraordinary a mark of
his Majefty's favour ; what was the price of
the patent he has bought, and to what honourable purpofe the purchafe-money has
been applied. Nothing lefs than many thou-
fands could pay Colonel Burgoyne's expences
at Prefton *. Do you dare to profecute fuch
a creature as Vaughan, while you are bafely fetting up the Royal Patronage to auc-
tion ? Do you dare to complain of an attack
upon your own honour, while you are felling
the favours of the crown, to raife a fund for
corrupting the morals of the people ? And,
do you think it poffible fuch enormities fhould
efcape without impeachment ? It is indeed
highly your intereft to maintain the prefent
houfe of commons. Having fold the nation
to you in grofs, they will undoubtedly protect
you in the detail ; for while they patronize
your crimes, they feel for their own.

JUNIUS.

---

* Expences of his election there. The Colonel
brought in his light dragoons to his affiftance, and
Prefton feemed like a town taken by ftorm. For his
behaviour at this election a fuit was brought againft
him, and he was fined 1000l.

LETTER

LETTER L.

TO HIS GRACE THE DUKE OF GRAFTON.

MY LORD,   12 *Dec.* 1769.

I FIND with fome furprife, that you are not fupported as you deferve. Your moft determined advocates have fcruples about them, which you are unacquainted with ; and, though there be nothing too hazardous for your Grace to engage in, there are fome things too infamous for the vileft proftitute of a news-paper to defend. In, what other manner fhall we account for the profound, fubmiffive filence, which you and your friends have obferved upon a charge, which called immediately for the cleareft refutation, and would have juftified the fevereft meafures of refentment? I did not attempt to blaft your character by an indirect, ambiguous infinuation, but candidly ftated to you a plain fact, which ftruck directly at the integrity of a privy counfellor, of a firft commiffioner of the treafury, and of a leading minifter, who is fuppofed to enjoy the firft fhare in his Majefty's confidence. In every one of thefe capacities I employed the moft moderate terms to charge you with

treachery

treachery to your Sovereign, and breach of truft in your office. I accufed you of having fold a patent place in the collection of the cuftoms at Exeter, to one Mr. Hine, who, unable or unwilling to depofit the whole purchafe-money himfelf, raifed part of it by contribution, and has now a certain Doctor Brooke quartered upon the falary for one hundred pounds a year.—No fale by the candle was ever conducted with greater formality—I affirm that the price, at which the place was knocked down (and which, I have good reafon to think, was not lefs than three thoufand five hundred pounds) was, with your connivance and confent, paid to Colonel Burgoyne, to reward him, I prefume, for the decency of his deportment at Prefton ; or to reimburfe him, perhaps, for the fine of one thoufand pounds, which, for that very deportment, the court of King's Bench thought proper to fet upon him.—It is not often that the chief juftice and the prime minifter are fo ftrangely at variance in their opinions of men and things.

I THANK God there is not in human nature a degree of impudence daring enough to deny the charge I have fixed upon you. Your courteous fecretary *, your confiden-

* THOMAS BRADSHAW.

tial

tial architect † are silent as the grave. Even
Mr. Rigby's countenance fails him. He vio-
lates his second nature, and blushes whenever he speaks of you.—Perhaps the noble
Colonel himself will relieve you. No man
is more tender of his reputation. He is not
only nice, but perfectly sore in every thing
that touches his honour. If any man, for
example, were to accuse him of taking his
stand at a gaming-table, and watching, with
the soberest attention, for a fair opportunity
of engaging a drunken young nobleman at
piquet, he would undoubtedly consider it as
an infamous aspersion upon his character,
and resent it like a man of honour.—Ac-
quitting him therefore of drawing a regular
and splendid subsistence from any unworthy
practices, either in his own house or else-
where, let me ask your Grace, for what military merits you have been pleased to reward
him with a military government? He had a
regiment of dragoons, which one would imagine, was at least an equivalent for any ser-
vices he ever performed. Besides, he is but a
young officer considering his preferment,
and, except in his activity at Preston, not very conspicuous in his profession. But it
seems, the sale of a civil employment was not

† Mr. Taylor and George Ross, the Scotch agent
and confidante of Lord Mansfield, are said to have
managed the business.

suf-

sufficient, and military governments, which were intended for the support of worn out veterans, muft be thrown into the fcale, to defray the extenfive bribery of a contefted election. Are thefe the fteps you take to fe-cure to your fovereign the attachment of his army ? With what countenance dare you ap-pear in the royal prefence, branded as you are with the infamy of a notorious breach of truft ? With what countenance can you take your feat at the treafury-board, or in council, when you feel that every circulating whifper is at your expence alone, and ftabs you to the heart ? Have you a fingle friend in parlia-ment fo fhamelefs, fo thoroughly abandoned, as to undertake your defence. You know, my Lord, that there is not a man in either houfe, whofe character, however flagitious, would not be ruined by mixing his reputa-tion with yours ; and does not your heart inform you, that you are degraded below the condition of a man, when you are obliged to hear thefe infults with fubmiffion, and even to thank me for my moderation ?

WE are told, by the higheft judicial au-thority, that Mr. Vaughan's offer to pur-chafe the reverfion of a patent in Jamaica (which he was otherwife fufficiently entitled to) amounted to a high mifdemeanour. Be it fo : and if he deferves it, let him be pu-nifhed

nifhed. But the learned judge might have had a fairer opportunity of difplaying the powers of his eloquence. Having delivered himfelf with fo much energy upon the criminal nature, and dangerous confequences of any attempt to corrupt a man in your Grace's ftation, what would he have faid to the minifter himfelf, to that very privy counfellor, to that firft commiffioner of the treafury, who does not wait for, but impatiently folicits the touch of corruption ; who employs the meaneft of his creatures in thefe honourable fervices, and, forgetting the genius and fidelity of his fecretary, defcends to apply to his houfe-builder for affiftance ?

THIS affair, my Lord, will do infinite credit to government, if, to clear your chatacter, you fhould think proper to bring it into the houfe of Lords, or into the court of King's Bench*.—But, my Lord, you dare not do either.

                                    J U N I U S.

* A SHORT time before the publication of the two preceding letters, the Duke of Grafton had commenced a profecution againft Mr. Samuel Vaughan, for attempting to corrupt him by an offer of 5000l. for a patent place in Jamaica. When the rule to fhew caufe, why an information fhould not be exhibited againft Vaughan, was argued in the King's Bench, Nov. 27th, 1769, by the opinion of the four judges, the rule was made abfolute. The following accurate extract from Lord Mansfield's
                                              fpeech

speech on the occasion, deserves attention. " A prac-
" tice of the kind complained of here is certainly dif-
" honourable and scandalous.—If a man, standing un-
" der the relation of an officer under the King, or of a
" person in whom the King puts confidence, or of a
" minister, takes money for the use of that confidence
" the King puts in him, he basely betrays the King,—
" he basely betrays his trust.—If the King sold the
" office, it would be acting contrary to the trust the
" constitution hath reposed in him. The constitution
" does not intend the crown should sell those offices, to
" raise a revenue out of them.—Is it possible to hesi-
" tate, whether this would not be criminal in the Duke
" of Grafton;—contrary to his duty as a privy coun-
" sellor;—contrary to his duty as a minister;—contrary
" to his duty as a subject?—His advice should be free
" according to his judgement;—It is the duty of his
" office;—he has sworn to it."—Notwithstanding this,
the Duke is positively said by Junius to have sold a patent place to Mr. Hine for 3500l. and yet was Lord
Privy Seal when this letter was written. If the house
of commons had impeached the Duke as they ought to
have done, Lord Mansfield would have been in a most
ridiculous situation. On Junius's discovery and publication of the Duke's conduct, the prosecution against
Vaughan was dropped, on purpose it is said to save
both the Judge and the Duke.

END OF VOLUME I.

www.ingramcontent.com/pod-product-compliance
Lightning Source LLC
Chambersburg PA
CBHW030348270326
41926CB00009B/1009